Into the Pleasure Dome

the films

of

Kenneth Anger

Edited by Jayne Pilling and Mike O'Pray

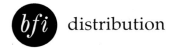 distribution

1989

Table of Contents

Kenneth Anger. Portrait by Teské.

INTRODUCTION

This dossier, and the season of films it accompanies, is a celebration of the films of Kenneth Anger - himself a living legend.

Renowned as the author of the infamous and scandalous best-selling book *Hollywood Babylon*, he is also a figure who continually generates rumours of bizarre practices, grandiose schemes and acerbic, idiosyncratic views.

Immersed in Hollywood's myth making at an early age as a child actor in Max Rheinhardt's *Midsummer Night's Dream* , by his teens he'd already become a prolific filmmaker of shorts: *Fireworks*, one of his greatest films, was made at the astonishing age of seventeen. The Anger myth can be ascribed to many things - his smouldering good looks; his involvement over the years with the world of magic, astrology, mythical knowledge and the pop world of Mick Jagger, Marianne Faithfull, Jimmy Page; the announcement of his own death in the pages of New York's Village Voice, the destruction and loss of his films, his self-exile to Europe where an early champion of his work was Jean Cocteau.

At the core of all this mythology is a film-maker of prodigious talent. The skill, imagination and visual force of such films as *Scorpio Rising*, *The Inauguration of the Pleasure Dome* and *Eaux d'artifice* has not been surpassed. Equally, his critique of aspects of American culture (movies, television, bike-gangs) in *Scorpio Rising* has influenced both the American and international avant-garde film movements and more mainstream film-makers of such stature as Martin Scorsese, David Lynch and R.W. Fassbinder. The ironic juxtaposition of popular music with the image track used so much nowadays in pop videos also shows his influence. His intense visual imagination aligned with music to form a poetics (shot through with wit and humour) of modern day life has been one of his major contributions to film. Anger's work (that which is extant) comprises little more than three hours: the durability of the films and their impact is thus all the more staggering.

This dossier owes its existence to the fact that the British Film Institute's Distribution Division has recently acquired brand new prints of Kenneth Anger's films, which are being showcased at the National Film Theatre in London in a season entitled 'Inside the Pleasure Dome', which then tours, in a modified version, round the network of Regional Film Theatres in the U.K., under the aegis of Film and Video Umbrella (jointly funded by the British Film Institute and the Arts Council of Great Britain). *The Guardian* newspaper is also to be thanked for support in bringing over Kenneth Anger for a 'Guardian Screen Event' at the NFT and Edinburgh's Filmhouse.

We would like to thank the following for advice and support for the contents of this dossier: Kenneth Anger, Tony Rayns, Ray Durgnat, David Wilson, Stephen Woolley, Martin Scorsese, and particular thanks to Rebekah Wood. For the production of the dossier we'd also like to thank Tricia Carrington, Barry Edson, John Smoker, Kathy Meldrum, Gill Crawford, Sally Dowden, and particularly Heather Stewart and Ania Witkowska for generously giving of their time and advice.

Jayne Pilling and Michael O'Pray.

Lucifer: a Kenneth Anger Kompendium

by Tony Rayns

1. STATEMENTS

I have always considered movies evil; the day that cinema was invented was a black day for mankind. Centuries before photography there were talismans, which actually anticipated photographs, since the dyes they used on the cheap vellum produced patterns when they faded in light. A talisman was a sticky flypaper trying to trap a spirit - cunningly you printed on it a 'photograph' of the demon you wanted to capture in it. Photography is a blatant attempt to steal the soul. The astral body is always just latent in a person, and certain cunning and gifted photographers can take an image of the astral body. The whole thing is having an image of someone to control them. If you're out of your mind with love, it becomes understandable. Any crime is justifiable in the name of Love. In fact, it shouldn't have to be a 'crime': Anything is justifiable in the name of Love.

My films are primarily concerned with sexuality in people. My reason for filming has nothing to do with 'cinema' at all; it's a transparent excuse for capturing people, the equivalent of saying 'Come up & see my etchings'... it's wearing a little thin now...So I consider myself as working Evil in an evil medium.

2. LORE

I am a non-prolific film-maker - the opposite of, say, Andy Warhol. I show very few of the films I have made...
Kenneth Anger has six films in distribution, representing some 22 years' filming: *Fireworks* (1947), *Eaux d'Artifice* (1953), *Inauguration of the Pleasure Dome* (1954-66,) *Scorpio Rising* (1964), *Kustom Kar Kommandos* (1965) and *Invocation of my Demon Brother* (also known as Zap, 1969). His earliest exhibited film was made at the age of 7, with the Boy Scouts - *Ferdinand the Bull*, later done as a cartoon by Disney. *I'd been in the Reinhardt* Midsummer Night's Dream, *mixing with Hollywood people, and so I knew what effeminate people were. In* Ferdinand *I had the bull (two boys under a skin) played effeminate...* His family owned a 16mm Kodak movie camera with a 100-foot load, used to film outings, and Anger would take end-scraps from those reels for films of his own. *Fireworks*, made at the age of 17, was shot in his Hollywood home on three nights when his parents were away, on film stock stolen from the US Navy (obviously, Anger doesn't regret this theft in the least, but he has since

been punished grossly disproportionately by thefts of his equipment and other property - in the case of the orginal 1966 *Lucifer Rising*, the film itself). Typically, Anger then began a massively over-ambitious project for a feature in colour called *Puce Women*, and completed only one sequence (*Puce Moment*) which he no longer distributes, but occasionally shows. Then Kodak labs confiscated the footage for a ritual film in colour called *The Love that Whirls*, because of nudity; and two subsequent projects that Anger began in France (with some assistance from Cocteau) failed for lack of means. A version of Cocteau's ballet *Le Jeune Homme et la Mort* which Anger filmed (with Roland Petit choreography) in a wintery garden in the absence of a set survives only in a b & w version, which cannot be shown for copyright reasons. In 1953 he brought off his first completed film for 6 years, *Eaux d'Artifice*, shot in the gardens of the Villa d'Este in Tivoli. In America in 1954 he shot the material for *Inauguration of the Pleasure Dome*, and prepared the original single-screen version, with its emphatically cyclic structure, using for soundtrack music by Harry Partch (to a 43-tone scale, played on instruments of his own invention: the cloud chamber, diamond marimba, chromelodeon and others). In 1955 he shot the short documentary account of Aleister Crowley's retreat in Cefalu,*Thelema Abbey*. He prepared the triple-screen version of *Pleasure Dome* (in which the main screen grew 'wings' at the movie's climax) for the 1958 Brussels EXPRML Festival, where it was run along with *Eaux d'Artifice*; *Pleasure Dome* in fact began a session that climaxed with Richard Williams' *The Little Island*, but despite this won the L'Age d'Or award. In Europe, Stan Brakhage filmed Anger as the only living person in his lament *The Dead*, feeling that the man's depressed frustration related to the moods he was creating in filming tombs. ' 59 to '61 Anger filmed the material for a version of the Olympia Press novel *L'Histoire d'O*, but never completed the movie because of both a characteristic over-ambitiousness and, apparently, harassment from the authorities. He returned to America (where Marie Menken shot her *Arabesque for*

Kenneth Anger), and made *Scorpio Rising* on ...
of which he was given a Ford Found...
completely breadless, and I consciensciously ...
the time I'd taken care of my debts, there w...
the $10,000... He began *Kustom Kar Kon...*
pleted only one sequence (now distribu...
from a work no longer in progress) bef...
out. '66 he began the 'Love Vision' *Lu...*
doned when the footage was stolen afte...
ing of a rough-cut. Anger publicly ren...
ing with a full-page In Memoriam in T...
and came to Britain to prepare the S...
Edition of *Inauguration of the Pleasure Do...*
Anger Aquarian Arcanum, a series of Ma...
Crowley paintings accompanied by Ku...
prologue for this, but has since dropped it. ...
year he completed a third editing of footag...
Francisco, and originally intended as Part ...
Rising, now shown as an 11-minute film *Invo...*
Demon Brother. He is now planning a new *Lucife...*
a full-length feature in colour, and a short Magic...
the Goddess Kali, using footage shot with frie...
recent trip to India, and additional footage to be s...
country.

Anger's films, always rigorous, have become i... easingly so as he has become more self-demanding. Everything in *Fireworks* was achieved in one take, that being the only film for which Anger has ever had a script. The editing ratio for *Scorpio* was around 5:1; that for *Invocation* was nearer 20:1 - the film having been through two (unshown) versions, and months of careful refinement.

3. IMAGE

The only film-makers Anger passionately admires are Sergei Eisenstein and D W Griffith; Griffith as the creator of mythic Hollywood, and builder of Babylon in Hollywood, and the man who developed and refined his films with each successive print. (Anger's book *Hollywood Baby-lon* concerns the cataclysmic decline of Hollywood from ...ith's splendour to today's effective write-off, pointing ... Star as the agent of the decline: *There was Venus and ...ly called Clara and Ruby; there was Pan called ...e was even old Bacchus named Fatty and maimed ... Lon. It was an illusion, a tease, a fraud; it was ... fun as the 'old-time religion' without blood on ... the blood would come ...* Eisenstein as the ...ost Maker; Rene Micha, writing about ...ps Modernes, pointed out the relationship: ...nceived in the complex sense desired by Eisen-...al, emotional, intellectual; to which is added ...van the Terrible) *a formidable surrealism.* ...nquestionably the world's foremost expo-...tage of attractions'. Co-incidentally, Eis-...aking career was as littered with broken ...r's has been.

The other Maker to have significantly affected Anger was, of course, Jean Cocteau. Cocteau's famous championship of *Fireworks* (*... comes from that beautiful night from which emerge all the true works. It touches the quick of the soul, and this is very rare*) complements the fact that Anger's film has close affinities with *Le Sang d'un Poete* - little direct borrow-ing (perhaps the white hand, and the journey beyond the door) but it's difficult to suggest two films with greater *textural* unity, notably in their respective openings - close-ups of the protagonist ill at ease in his environment, and in front of his own reflection. *Orphee*'s tangle of life, love and death, and its motorcyclist iconography obviously lead towards *Scorpio Rising*. Curiously, and probably co-inci-dentally, some of Cocteau's characters in *Sang d'un Poete* look quite strikingly like Shiva and Kali in *Pleasure Dome*. And *Lucifer Rising*, if Anger can finally release it, will be his *Testament d'Orphee*.

Aside from these, Anger's stated preference is for horror and fantasy cinema: *I have my favorite serials which I've seen over and over: Flash Gordon, Daredevils of the Red Circle, Chandu. That, and the kind of little B film they used to make at Warner's and Columbia... The horror film is a great form; it's a kind of nightmare wonderland...**In conversation, Anger will frequently refer to a Thirties Hollywood fantasy for a point of reference. It is notable that such a film as Victor Halperin's *White Zombie* touches thematically on many of Anger's preoccupations.

4. FILM FORM

I like the idea that an experience can be put in a can and somebody can recreate it. But when I work on a film I don't think I could ever worry about whether people will like or understand it. when I really get into that creative thing of making a movie, it's just me, and the camera, and whatever else happens to be there*.

Anger has an amazing instinctive grasp of all the elements of film-making; his films actively work out much of Eisen-stein's theoretical writing about the cinema. For instance, Esenstein's ideal of chromophonic (colour/sound) mon-tage, described in *The Film Sense*, is startingly achieved in the 'party lights' sequence in *Scorpio Rising*, where the Randells' hard, dense arrangements of song - for the first time in the movie, cutting in before the end of the preced-ing song - is matched by a thickening in the terms of reference in the montage, while at the same time the lyrics relate explicitly to the film's development of its colour scale. Equally, the tightly controlled pastel colours of *Kustom Kar Kommandos* perfectly match the 'pastel' ar-rangement of 'Dream Lover' for the Parris Sisters. Self-evidently, this is not chromophonic montage in Eisen-tein's lofty sense, but it comes nearer than anything in commercial cinema, and produces film-making as rich in resonance as anything of Eisenstein's own.

Fascinatingly, Anger plans to use another of Eisenstein's theories in making *Lucifer Rising*: he wants to explore the possibilities of vertical composition. In his crucial essay

The Dynamic Square Eisenstein complains that the advent of CinemaScope cripples yet further the adventurous film-maker's chances of breaking away from the limitations of passive horizontal composition: *It is my purpose to defend the cause of the 50% of compositional possibilities which have been banished from the light of the screen. It is my desire to chant the hymn of the male, the strong, the virile, active, vertical composition! I am not anxious to enter into the dark phallic and sexual ancestry of the* vertical *shape as a symbol of growth, strength or power...* Naturally enough, this precisely *is* Anger's desire: *I guess my whole trip is phallic worship...*

5. ALLEGORY OF LUCIFER

As far back as Kenneth Anger remembers, he's been 'on a fire/light trip'. He recalls being a minor childhood arsonist (*Nothing big - a few fields...and a church*), and he once built a miniature volcano in the family backyard for a science-fiction puppet called *Prisoner of Mars*. Light is central to his films. The opening narration of *Fireworks* states the thesis: *Inflammable desires dampened by day under the cold water of consciousness are ignited at night by the libertarian matches of sleep and burst forth in showers of shimmering incandescence....,* illustrated in the opening shot of the film, a flash-frame of a phallic fire-brand thrust into turbulent water, which is repeated directly after the famous climax with a phallic Roman Candle in orgasm. The Dreamer (Anger himself) goes out in the night seeking 'a light' but finds at first only the stark lights of night traffic on a freeway. He faces the crunch by asking a sailor for a light for his cigarette (the first of several pointed cigarette-lightings in Anger films) which, after a brief taste of the violence to come, he gets in the form of a bundle of flaming branches from a grate. Those flames burn emotionally through the rest of the film, burning out only when the photographs of the beginning of the Dream have smouldered away. There, the fire purifies by burning; the hand with severed fingers (which at the start of the film stands for the Dreamer's stunted

The dream....

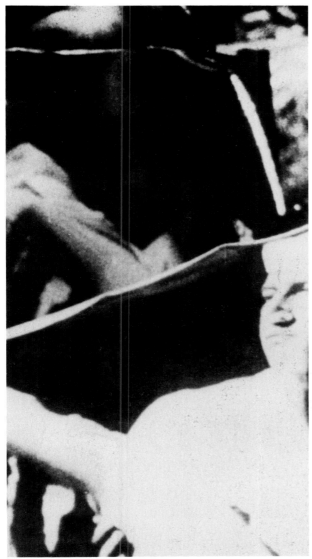

....burns. Kenneth Anger and Gordon Gray in *Fireworks*.

adolescence, and which is visually compared with the stubs in an empty book of matches) is restored to wholeness at the end of the film, when the ritual has been braved and endured.

Fire is a major part of the element of control in *Inauguration of the Pleasure Dome*. Lilith, the first guest to arrive at Shiva's convocation, is 'born of flame' in a triple-dissolve amongst the most flawless in the history of montage, but she 'burns' in the superimposed red flames (from Harry Lachman's staggering *Dante's Inferno*) with her fellow-guests when Shiva assumes control. Kali, on the other hand, controls fire from the moment she lights her joint by drawing flame from the tiny horned figure of a devil; and it is she at the end who 'blesses the Rites of the Children of the Light while Shiva evokes the godhead with the formula Force and Fire ', her image persisting through the visual delirium of the finale. Like her, Scorpio creates his own fire - by striking a match on his teeth to light his cigarette.

The power of Light is the explicit object of *Invocation of my Demon Brother*: the shadowing forth of Our Lord Lucifer. The dance of the Magus widdershins around the Swirling Spiral Force, the solar swastika, until the Bringer of Light - Lucifer - breaks through. Even in the Anger films in which Light plays no evident part in the action, it is of note: in *Eaux d'Artifice* (as the title suggests, it's the converse of *Fireworks*), Light is conspicuous by its absence, which is part of the film's satiric purpose. Equally, it's no accident that Anger's filmic tarot card *Kustom Kar Kommandos*, a view of the 7th trump, the Charioteer, should prove to have the Title: The Lord of the Triumph of Light.

666 MAGICK

The science and art of causing change to occur in conformity with the Will. Magick is the Science of understanding oneself and one's conditions. It is the Art of applying that understanding in action. - Aleister Crowley.

9

Kenneth Anger is a follower of the English occultist Aleister Crowley, who designated his work Magick, deliberately choosing a discredited term and swearing to rehabilitate it. The fundamental precepts and workings of Magick are set out most accessibly (in every sense) in Crowley's major work *Magick in Theory and Practice*, and it would be foolish and presumptuous to attempt to summarise them here. Anger is totally committed to Magick (and is indeed increasingly inclined to regard his occult work as more important than the films) and so, naturally, it informs the films he makes. Which is not to say that the movies are esoteric mysteries, impenetrable to non-followers of Crowley's line, but simply that the viewer who comes to them with some awareness of what Magick is about will have a sharper understanding of why Anger made them the way he did. At the lowest level: the viewer of *Scorpio Rising* alert to Magick will notice (eventually) the tiny shot in the rally scenes near the end of the movie where Anger zooms in on a motorcycle numbered 777, and will recognise this as a Magickal reference, since 777 is the number Title of one of the most important Magick manuals, a table of correspondances from the Qabalah. 'Seeing' this fleeting, unemphasised shot (joke? comment? Magick coincidence?) is rather different from, say, recognising an in-joke in early Godard; the viewer who 'sees' it understands better the way Anger put the sequence together. On a higher level: the viewer who recognises that *Fireworks* corresponds to the Magick ritual The Building of the Pyramid (a process of self-initiation, in which the candidate confesses) will appreciate more keenly what the film meant and means to Anger. Anger's increasingly dominant concern with Magick is reflected in *Invocation of my Demon Brother*, which limits its terms of reference almost exclusively to Magick ritual, and which will thus inevitably perplex the viewer who expects to comprehend the meaning of actions outside the context of the movie he's seeing them in. But Anger, unassailable in his confidence in Magick, knows (as he did with *Pleasure Dome*) that the movie works, that it will affect any audience long before they consciously understand it.

For the record, in Anger's own words: *The Age that ended in 1962 was the Piscean Age, the Age of the Fish, which was the Age of Jesus Christ. Where the Piscean Age was ruled by Neptune, the planet of mysticism, the Aquarian Age is ruled by Uranus, the most erratic planet of all... it's the sign of the unexpected, revolution, for one thing... the last 2000 years were based on renunciation, sacrifice, and guilt. The fight for the next generation, the next 25 years, 50 years, just the beginning of the fight really, is skinning off the shell that's left over from the last era**

In the films, Anger uses 'astrology like color. I use it in a poetic sense'. Thus *Scorpio Rising* dramatises the tensions between the powers of the dying Piscean Age and the Scorpions of the incoming Aquarian Age, though the precise terms of reference of the film are governed by Anger's interest and tastes. This gives the lie to Ronald Tavel's sadly weak attack on Anger (in his essay 'Shortcomings of the Sexual Metaphor in New York's Independent Films,' collected in Gregory Battcock's anthology *The New American Cinema*, Dutton 1967); Tavel ignores the fact that a system of astrology is simply a means of classifying 'the numberless possibilities which lie open to us', and fails to observe the breathtaking freedom of invention that typifies Anger's films. As even a pop astrologer (the kind reviled by Crowley) knows, Aquarian people love humanity, not in a Sagittarian way (personal love) but rather they love the life principle. To the Aquarian, the fact that there is life makes all things possible. Anger is an Aquarian.

7. THE MAGICK LANTERN CYCLE

Fireworks, like Kenneth Anger's other early films, was made primarily because it fulfilled a need - these imaginary displays provide a temporary release . Harry Smith, in his interview with P. Adams Sitney (Film Culture 37, also collected in Battcock's book), describes Anger at home at this time, and also how he (Smith) arranged the first large public screening of the movie. *As a child I felt a terrible need for love, and there was a terrible lack. My family offered nothing, and so I found it vicariously in violence. There's a strain of violence all through my films.* In *Fireworks*, Anger plays himself coming to terms with his developing identity - a Dreamer who is 'drawn through the needle's eye', and realises his dreams. It is constructed with luminous clarity (Terry Southern calls it the most perfectly structured film he's seen): the start of the Dream is a vision of the Dreamer bloody and inert in the arms of a sailor - a passive victim; and after the ordeal photographs of this scene catch fire and burn away. Complementarily, an early shot in the movie, a pan down the wall of the room to the Dreamer alone in bed and then on to the broken form of a white hand in the foreground, is repeated exactly at the end of the film, but with another (faceless) boy in bed with him, and the hand repaired.

The development of the main part of the film is too direct to require analysis; no audience is immune to its convulsive violence. Worth pointing out, though, is the way that *Fireworks* established several important motifs for future films. Most interesting is the Dreamer's waking at the star; all Anger's films begin either with the act of waking, or a metaphor for it. This suggests more simply and forcefully than any other image I have come across the autonomous life of the film as an active experience when it is being projected. It relates explicitly to the theme of film as ritual, as, in the case of *Fireworks*, does the soundtrack: thunder before the music, to clear the air.... The waking is followed by the (ritual) act of dressing, an assumption of identity. In *Fireworks*, the Dreamer dresses anonymously in white shirt and black pants, hesitantly and fumblingly his anxieties crystalised in the image of the broken hand. The theme is worked through: the sailors (in uniform, a group) rip the Dreamer's clothes off, and he undergoes the trial naked; but after the ordeal, and the extremely beautiful images of milk flowing like balm over the bloody flesh, the Dreamer is seen stirring from the floor of the urinal, wearing a sailor's cap. The sailor of the prologue is seen again in his Roman Candle orgasm, and the Dreamer metamorphoses into a Christmas tree in ironic ecstacy; and is finally back in his bed 'less empty than before', naked but not alone.

Other motifs introduced in *Fireworks* are the cigarette (taken up with Kali's and Scorpio's and prototype of the fan in *Eaux d'Artifice* and the Wand in *Invocation*) and the theme, crucial in *Pleasure Dome* and *Scorpio*, of an individual bending others to his Will: though the Dreamer is the sailor's victim, and they constitute the group from which his is excluded, they are his agents in the ritual of self-initiation, and when they have served their purpose they simply disappear, subsumed into the Dreamer's new-found strength. *Fireworks* also establishes the cyclic structure that dominates all the films up to *Kustom Kar Kommandos*: a ritual begun, developed, and achieved, infinitely repeatable, with the Maker's batteries charged a little higher each time. All Kenneth Anger's films gain increasingly with repeated viewings.

Eaux d'Artifice retells *Fireworks* in opposite terms. The Lady enters the 'night-time labyrinth of cascades, balustrades, grottoes and fountains', and tries to lure out the monsters with her fan; she's trying to invoke the water gods. Anger's own happy analogy is a middle-aged queen cruising for rough trade. She fails, being weak and frivolous, and melts into the water (surrenders her identity) so that she can play on.

Anger's grandmother was a costume mistress in silent films, and it was she who, working with Reinhardt, got Kenneth into the 1935 *Midsummer Night's Dream*. In his early youth Anger used to love dressing up in her costumes ('my transvestite period') and it was this that inspired the costume in *Eaux d'Artifice*, worn there by a circus dwarf Anger met in Italy. The Lady ('a Firbank

11

heroine in pursuit of a nightmoth') owes her plumes to Anger's Reinhardt costume, and her light-headedness to her past in Anger's childhood.

For all its (high) satiric content, *Eaux d'Artifice* is 'romance in the highest sense'. Its pace is leisured, its action timeless, its texture exquisite. The form is journey: at the start, the Lady revolves under the fountain she wants to own, and at the end she leaves the garden for a cold, dry world, leaving that fountain far behind in the distance. In between, her fluttering progress is cheerfully observed, tripping daintily through the supremely elaborate water-works that so effortlessly dominate her. Eventually she reaches the great stairway, and descends it in excited diagonals, while the water gods (cut-ins) watch threateningly. At the bottom, she spreads her (hand-tinted) fan, but without success - and she passively allows herself to be subsumed into the fountains, the image prefiguring its opposite, when Sandy merges into Buggy in *KKK*. Here, *Fireworks'* 'cold water of consciousness' becomes a gushing trip of its own, phallically spurring in Anger's most formally completely observed dream world.

Inauguration of the Pleasure Dome is full-scale ritual, to invoke Horus, the Crowned and Conquering Child, the Godhead of the Aquarian Age. It takes the form of a party. hosted by the Magician, in the guise of Lord Shiva, and his Scarlet Woman, Whore of Heaven, as Lady Kali. Their guests arrive in the guise of figures from mythology: Lilith, Isis, another woman, and then Pan, and then Astarte. The catalyst is Yage, Wormwood Brew, stolen from Hecate and served by Cesare the somnambulist (from *Caligari*). Lord Shiva venoms Pan's drink, and the Orgia ensues: a Magick masquerade party at which Pan is the prize...

Pleasure Dome is a vision of the Divine. Its most important element is control, and the control is Shiva's; he manipulates the guests from the moment they arrive, bearing their gifts, and has a different persona to receive each - from Osiris (to receive Isis; Golden Serpent) to Nero (to accept the Bunch of Bacchus from Pan). For the party, though, Shiva is resplendent in phallic headdress as the Great Beast 666, and as such he works on his guests till he exults in the consummation of the ritual as they abandon their individual identities. Shiva's gesture of consummation is the meeting of his open hands in an arc, and this image, constantly repeated, is the only stable element in the frenetic superimpositions of the movie's lengthy climax; in superimposition, it is as if Shiva is subsuming the others' passions into himself, and this is the key to the film: the disparate elements in the game, as moulded by Shiva, come together in Him, who repeats the ritual infinitely (continuous performances...) until He becomes God. Crowley speaks of this in *Magick in Theory and Practice: A Eucharist...is of more importance than any other magical ceremony, because it is a complete circle. The whole of the force expended is completely reabsorbed, yet the virtue is that vast gain represented by the abyss between Man and God.*

Pleasure Dome is so rich that little justice can be done it in so brief a piece as this. Like certain of Yeats' later plays (*The Herne's Egg*) it balances confidently between the most profound and the farcical, often using both at once: as in the arrival of Astarte (played literally radiantly by Anais Nin), first shedding a wrap yards long, and then in an aura of moonlight very beautifully magnifying her Gift of a Golden Sphere before presenting it to Shiva, who sprouts the Wings of Snow and flutters in delight like a Boy in Fairyland. The use of character-types is precise: Lilith has the pouting erotism of a Fifties cover girl, shocked when Shiva spurns her gift; Pan (played by Paul Mathison, who also painted the main title) is gorgeous beyond words, his expression glittering with evil self-interest and / or lechery when Astarte enters, and suffering most later in Shiva's manipulation of events; the painter Cameron remarkable as Kali, aloofly observing, and intervening only when Shiva gets a little too much into the swing of things, chinking goblets like champagne glasses with Lilith; Curtis

Harrington as Cesare, eloquently silent (the part having great resonances in his own films: Cameron and Mathison were involved in *Night Tide* and *Games* has several explicit quotes from Anger's film); and Anger himself the most physically expressive, as Hecate gyrating in fury at the theft of the Sacred Mushroom. In preparing the 1966 Sacred Mushroom Edition, Anger gave the movie a new track: Janacek's *Glagolitic Mass*, which like the songs in *Scorpio* is inseparable from the movie once you've seen it. *Scorpio Rising* uses the same cyclic structure, and a similar form of ritual, with a number of disparate elements coming together in the experience of the central protagonist. It begins as a conjuration of the Presiding Princes, Angels and Spirits of MARS with short, timeless sequences devoted to the motorcyclers waking (of course), dressing (of course), and working on their Machines. This movement

Shiva venoms Pan's drink: the turning point in *Inauguration of the Pleasure Dome*. Paul Mathison and Samson de Brier.

Inauguration of the Pleasure Dome

culminates in the introduction to Scorpio himself ('You look like an Angel...but you're the Devil in disguise'), who gets up, turns on, and then goes out to desecrate a church, while the other cyclers have a Hallowe'en party, and yet others ride rallies in the open country. In the church, Scorpio urinates into his helmet, and consecrates it; immediately he becomes his Demon Brother (black-masked, sub-machine-gun toting) while the Word is made Flesh in a curious death-totem/idol like a skeleton in a pressure suit (which reappears in Invocation). Scorpio in the church has a (brilliantly montage-based) rapport with the cyclers on their rally, and his Demon engineers a crash in which the cycler dies...The film moves from waking (the first shot, like the opening of *Endgame*, is a removal of a dustcover, which is a metaphor for the same thing) to death; and its cycle is achieved in a world of the red of mortality (the main title to the flashing red light of the end), comprehending death and initiation.

The structure is simple; the terms of reference are complex. In *Boys and Bolts*, the first part, the contrast is with a kid playing with his toy Police cyclers, wearing a 'I Was Born to Raise Hell' button which reappears on Scorpio's wall (suffer the little children....) which calls to mind incidentally Anger's early puppet films. In *Image Maker* the contrast is with Brando in meticulously selected snippets from *The Wild One* (precisely the kind of 'social' movie that Anger isn't making), with the aura of James Dean as a complement and a corrective. In *Walpurgis Party*, the contrast is with Christ ('J.C.Wallflower at the Cycler's Sabbath'), who exists in a pallid blue alien world of vague 'eternal longings'. And in *Rebel Rouser* the contrast is with Hitler, the autocrat bending masses to his Will, but to perverted, impersonal ends. The powers of ther Piscean Age are brought up to the rising sign of Scorpio in the Aquarian Age, and found wanting.....

The ritual, then, is Scorpio's; when he moves into overdrive in the final Wipeout sequence he becomes Thanatos ('in chrome and black leather and bursting jeans'). Unlike Shiva's, his ritual includes death; as a scorpion he stings. One guy shows at the Hallowe'en party as a skeleton with his prick hanging out - an astonishing image of virility in death; the cycle is necessarily violent to the point of death - it has to be that extreme to break away from the past. Initiation is seen as a kind of jokey reprise of *Fireworks*, but with really agonised electric screams on the track. Scorpio is the cycler who dies, but he also lives to carry out the ritual again. As it develops, the movie explores fascinating tensions between *Scorpio Rising* and Descending: the super-butch men of the early sequences give way to the frivolous guys playing around at the party, just as the 'monumental' sequences in which they are celebrated give way to the greater narrative flow of the later sequences; and the beautiful machines they cherish (at their best in the brilliant Taurus sequence,where John Sapienza puts the saddles on his Machine under the eye of the Reaper) give way to ordinary rally cycles. The decline on one level counterpoints Scorpio's personal ascendancy, but the tensions are richly resonant: as Scorpio flags the rally cyclers from the church altar (at the end of *Point of No Return*) behind the deathshead flag is seen the scorpion: rising, descending, rising, descending, descending...

Kustom Kar Kommandos evokes the Dream Lover, but as a blind for the Charioteer of the Tarot Trumps. Infinitely more subtly, it restates the theme of *Fireworks*; it is about the simultaneous longing for, and illusory attainment of an ideal. Anger's camera, gliding with the delicacy of a scrap of down, caresses the All Chrome Ruby Plush Dream Buggy, and then Sandy, the Maker, who in turn caresses it with a giant white powder puff. The images are suffused with a pink glow from the background, the Maker appears in complementary azure. The film starts with a 'waking' image of the Kar door opening into the camera, to show the Scorpio red inside, and then moves through ten lingering, indefinable dissolves which completely circle the Kar, eventually returning to the original shot, but with the

Maker this time getting into the Kar, settling and driving off. The images centre on the powder puff, twice brushed by tiny erotic gusts, the incarnation of the spirit of the movie: very campy, but also achingly precarious. In a hallucinatory shot of Sandy's reflection on the inside of the passenger Kar door, there is a moment of fusion - the colour elements (pink, azure, red, and the dull amber of the Kar itself) fuse, and Maker and Kar are one. The final shot of the sequence shows his face, serene, impassive, moving as if directed by some non-conscious force; he drives off. 'Every night I hope and pray a Dream Lover will come my way...'

Invocation of My Demon Brother is a fast moving, very concentrated collage of Magick elements, in effect like the last thirty seconds of Scorpio extended to ten minutes. Anger calls it 'my most out-front film'. A satyr pipes (an equivalent to the three knocks at the start of the *Acquarian Arcanum* which Anger used as a prologue to *Pleasure Dome*, but has now dropped) and the Wand-bearer *wakes* to begin the ritual: a Midnight Mass where the Powers of Darkness gather to 'shadow forth' Lucifer. Kenneth Anger himself as the Magus, his face black and gold, great flowing robe, bathed in red light, dances with passionate energy widdershins (anti-sunwise) around the Swirling Spiral Force, the solar swastika. The Powers: the Acolyte, the Brother and Sister of the Rainbow, His Satanic Majesty, assist and participate. Joke: a hurried procession down the stairs, but a scorpion sting in the tail: 'ZAP You're pregnant - that's witchcraft'. Pause: the Magus with a copy of Crowley's novel *Moonchild*. Renewed force: flame, and a cremation. The Magus dances, is triumphant, exults, the solar swastika in one hand, flaming script in the other. And Lucifer breaks through....

Cut-ins: the Wand Bearer observing (Speed Hacker amazing with snow-white hair and eyebrows, caught in the light); two boys, first watching, then wrestling (*I was in Sacramento and I put up these two boy surfers who'd run away*

- *one negro, one white . They were great buddies - they swore eternal friendship while they stayed.....I filmed them....I risked fifty years in jail for putting them up for the night);* most important, US Marines jumping out of their helicopter in Vietnam. The movie was made on A, B and C rolls, and the C roll throughout is this one image made into a loop, so there's a continuous flow of men out of the helicopter. Mostly it's invisibly faint (Anger thinks it might be seen with infra-red glasses), twice it's there by itelf: a dozen men jumping out to face a death-situation just off-screen. Anger uses it as an image of anxiety; there's an urgency about it, in the stance of the bodies. *They're squares, enjoying the only kind of peak exposure they'll ever know.* Anger believes that audiences will sense the flow of men through the film, even when they can't see them.

Invocation is a film with rough edges. There is minimal visual flow - every cut hurts. Thence its fabulous power. Technically, it's even more ambitious than *Pleasure Dome*; fast motion (giving the Magus' dance frightening, demonic energy), stills, multiple imposition. For the first time, Anger has an original soundtrack, composed on Moog synthesiser by Mick Jagger (the Stones' song *Sympathy for the Devil* was partly inspired by Anger); Anger calls it 'an attack on the sensorium'. Amongst many virtuoso shots, Anger has realised for himself a photograph of the Beatles he once admired, in which it appeared Ringo had eight arms; Anger superimposes a figure on himself upside-down (like a playing card), and adds other arms. The final shots of the movie, with their pale, flickering Light, are unlike anything he has shown before.

The true magic of Horus requires the passionate union of opposites (Crowley); *Invocation* is founded on a clash between the circle and the swastika ('a psychic power pack - Hitler couldn't have done it without the swastika'). The circle takes various forms: the circle of the Magus' dance, the black musicians' circle, the whirling helicopter blades. Unifying, all through, is the pentagram: either in straight

16

superimposition, or on the helicopter, or in the patches of shadow, or in the angle at which characters position themselves. The image of the Marines gains force when one remembers that WW2 was a matter of US pentagrams versus German swastikas.

8 LUCIFER RISING

Lucifer is a Demon. A Demon of beauty, *which doesn't mean he doesn't still cause trouble. But then, nothing* really *causes trouble......*

The majority of the quotations from Kenneth Anger in this feature are taken from a conversation with Tony Rayns on 21 July 1969. Those asterisked (*) are taken from the only previously published Anger interview, in *Spider* magazine, reprinted in *Film Culture* . I am grateful to many friends for discussion of Anger's films; particularly Alan Spaderman and Jeff Stern.

First published in *Cinema* , No. 4, October, 1969.

[This article was written twenty years ago and no longer necessarily represents Tony Rayn's current thinking on Anger and his films].

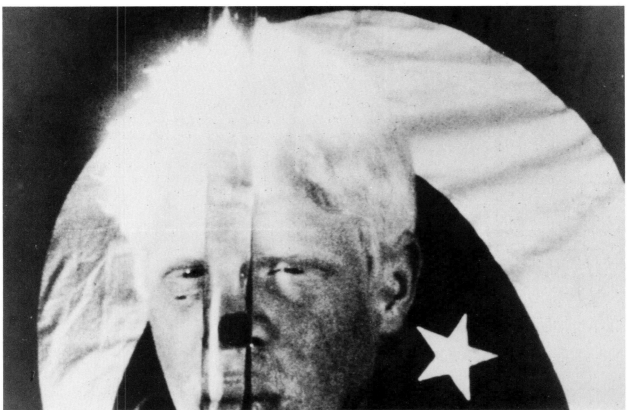

Invocation of my Demon Brother

MODESTY AND THE ART OF FILM
by Kenneth Anger

Up to now, poetry has followed a wrong course: rising to the heavens or crawling along the ground, it has ignored the principles of its existence and, not without reason, has constantly been rebuffed by decent people. It has not been modest... the finest quality that ought to exist in an imperfect being.
-Lautreamont, Les Chants de Maldoror

'Capturing the immediate moment' is unquestionably the principal condition of artistic creation. The poet who can seize the first spark of his inspiration at the very second it strikes and preserve it on the back of an envelope with the stub of a pencil; the native who because he is happily in love takes a bit of clay from the river bank and a few minutes later leaves an insouciant divinity to dry in the sun... how we envy them, those of us who work with film.

The problem, for every artist, is to hold this reflection of the divine fire of inspiration in the direction and the essence of his work, since he well knows how this transient fire, this flash of light which appears out of the night and has to be given expression - and yet which sometimes has the incandescent force of a newly born volcano - is a fragile thing: a witch's light, St Elmo's fire.
What Eisenstein called 'the first vision'.
What a strange paradox, then, is the film medium, that magnificent and terrible instrument born of our time to tempt and torture our creative imagination. Without in any way lessening our enthusiam for it as an art form, I don't think we - the children of this era - are wrong to call it an imperfect medium...imperfect and terrifying.

Let us look quite honestly for a moment at some of these imperfections, at once trivial and monumental, while never forgetting the specificity of an art in which the smallest speck of dust can quickly assume the menacing proportions of the Rock of Gibraltar.

Every artistic discipline needs its tools in the finest condition. Taken separately, those of the cinema have a capricious fragility: they have to be adjusted and handled with extreme care; they are not at all suited to untidy minds. Considerable scientific knowledge is recommended before going near these machines... which are also depressingly heavy, large and inflexible and need great strength to handle. They are all so interconnected that the slightest mistake in the procedure from the movement of the camera which unwinds the virgin film stock to the setting of the projectionist's arc lamp - can ruin the whole enterprise.

To master the complications which these machines present, the film-maker inevitably has to accept the collaboration of assistants, advisers, technicians...something that is more difficult to handle than the machine themselves: individual personalities. The actual material - film - has to be handled with care, because it can quickly be destroyed or irreparably damaged by a change in temperature, a chemical defect, or simply by oil, dirt or dust. Finally, this means of expression is the costliest ever. The artist cannot avoid taking into account that anti-poetic object - *finance* and that incomprehensible being the *financier*, who is forever invariably and unforgivably asking the same question: *why?*

Of course, we force ourselves to overcome these imperfections and to accept them as the challenge thrown down by this age of technology, since above all else we love cinema. These difficulties can in no way lessen the attraction of this promise of immortality, this certainty that there finally exists a mirror held up to the fleeting face of nature, a means of holding on to 'the inexhaustible flow of visions of beauty' which endlessly die and are reborn and which make of the contemplation of beauty a feeling imbued by the sadness of its disappearance, a way of holding on to the moment, a weapon with which to challenge the implacable unfolding of time - there is the miracle, the true miracle of film.

Breaking through the barrier of these mechanical shortcomings can only be achieved by a conscious return to simplicity, to the direct relationship between the camera and the artist.

The widespread idea that films necessarily involve the complex farce of the commercial cinema has its antithesis in a field of Japanese rice, where Okamoto wades in with a 16mm camera in his hand and achieves a totally different creative result. This Japanese film poet cut himself off from the script department, the studio, projectors, film crews and even the camera tripod, and went off by himself into the countryside in pursuit of his celluloid poems. His wonderful visual 'silent songs' - intimate and totally free - elicit my unbounded admiration. There is even an additional poetry in these slightly flickering images that are freed from all contingencies. Heir to a culture traditionally enamoured of the small and the refined, this poet does not scorn the 16mm camera, considering its lightness and its small size to be every bit to his advantage. He started out with an 8mm camera, and had it existed he would have used a 4mm camera. The dream of a personal, free, pure cinema can be fulfilled as long as you are modest.

Using the simplest of means of an art with lyrical associations is the very basis of the Japanese aesthetic and my own most precious memory of that culture. I shall never forget how the lesson was taught me, when I was a child, by my Japanese drawing teacher.

I had done a sketch of a seascape, a holiday memory, on which I'd worked laboriously and I took it to my master for criticism. He looked calmly at my grimy 'Western' page, on which in my enthusiasm I'd tried to put everything I had seen, and then with a slight smile he took a sheet of rice paper, dipped his brush in the ink, and in a flash there before me was the essence of the scene: three brush strokes, the outline of Mount Fuji, the island and its pine trees, the sweep of the bay.

This Japanese love for economy of expression is found in *tanka*, poems in five lines, and in *haiku*, which have a mere three lines.

Mastery of these forms of expression is regarded as the highest literary aspiration. The story is often told of the pupil who had composed the following haiku:

> *Clipping the wings*
> *of a flying dragon*
> *is pepper dust.**

To which his master replied:

> *Pepper dust*
> *Give it wings*
> *It's a flying dragon.*

A magical evocation born out of the rigours of choice. In their extreme limitation some forms have the suggestive force of an echo resonating endlessly in the imagination. Witness this brilliant example by the classical master Bashu:

> *What a piercing cold I feel.*
> *The comb of my deceased wife on the floor of the room*
> *Under my heel.*

---

*Literally, 'a peppercorn', i.e a futile exercise.

Western poets could profit from such an exercise of discipline, just as we film-makers might bear in mind the lesson of Okamoto's films, which evoke in two or three images of high lyricism the poignant drama of an orphan, an aquatic flower, devotion to a doll or to a 'perfect friendship'.

Let's give our Western poets the opportunity to reflect on the possibilities offered by three lines, by three brush strokes, and - for our film poets - by three images. The result may well be surprising.

In contrast to this art of lyrical evocation, the Western tradition - from Michelangelo to Griffith via Beethoven - most often aspires to the grandiose, the epic, to the 'big'. Though of the works of these artists it is not the 'smaller scale', more poetic, more personal ones that we cherish most: we don't prefer Michelangelo's sonnets to the Sistine Chapel, Beethoven's quartets to his symphonies, *Broken Blossoms* to *Intolerance*.

We admire the epic, but we are moved by the lyrical. This is even more evidently the case with comedy. What better example than the crystallisation of the meaning of improvisation in Keaton or Chaplin - a meaning which, in the field of cinema, already belongs to a 'lost art'. It is the improvised moments that remain the most precious.

In the art of film, the divine spark of intuition very quickly arouses the desire for total control. The studied composition of the epic leads us to the 'frozen realms' of Eisenstein and late-period Dreyer, Sternberg and Bresson. We admire the formal beauty of these works but their coldness fails to move us. The spectator must 'appreciate' the quality of these works before 'feeling' them, competently analyse the ingenuity of the camera movements and the merits of the lighting before being involved in the action. The veil of judgment is drawn between the spectator and the drama.

Since it is now an imperative of the film industry that a film must be carefully prepared, designed and rehearsed in advance to avoid financial disaster, it is not surprising that the 'greats' of cinema have tried to overcome these complications through a rigid intellectual control. But these proceedings increasingly take the form of rites, and in sacrificing freedom and spontaneity in this way the 'icy masters' have at the same time stifled audience 'response'. Their works are increasingly becoming 'ends in themselves' exercises in highly refined style, but they lack the irreplaceable qualities of improvisation.

Looking at the work of these film intellectuals, we find ourselves watching something where concern for perfection of detail and nuance has led to the film-maker betraying the motivations and the object of the drama. The dynamic elements of the dramatic structure have been ousted, the flow of emotions dissipated, and with every gesture and every shadow becoming more perfect the rhythm gets progessively slower until the film is no more than a carefully studied series of vignettes. The initial value as drama, the power of catharsis, is lost.

Note also the growing tendency in today's commercial films to break the action up into 'frames' or flashbacks, often accompanied by the inopportune presence of a commentary whose superimposition on the visual action constantly means us having to switch from the realm of the immediate to that of nostalgia for the past. To put it another way, the film-maker is saying 'This happened' or 'This happened to me' rather than the vital 'This is happening ' or 'I am'.

This widespread neutralising of the essential point of cinema - its power to simulate real experience - enshrines its more off-putting tendency. So we are now in the cul-de-sac of stylisation. From the mouths of the half-dead people who pronounce the oracles of the contemporary screen should come a freedom charter: the restoration of the persuasive poetics of the lyrical image. A freedom that is only possible through the artist's intimate view through the lens of his camera, in a word through 'personal cinema'.

It was precisely this 'cinematic' potential for expressing spontaneity that attracted me as a form of personal art. I saw its disruptive strength: a way of bringing about a change. This means of expression can transcend the aesthetic to become experience. My ideal was a 'living' cinema that explored the dynamism of the visual communication of beauty, fear and joy. I wanted my personal cinema to transmute the dance of my interior being into a poetry of moving images that would create a new climate of spiritual revelation where the spectator, forgetting that he or she was looking at a work of art, could only become one with the drama. I knew that an art like this needed only the simplest of means: Okamoto and the lesson of Japanese aesthetics had shown me the way.

With a hand-held 16mm camera I shot my first series of short haiku. This was my apprenticeship in the marvels that surround us, waiting to be discovered, awake to knowledge and life and whose magical essence is revealed by selection. At seventeen, I composed my first long poem, a fifteen minute suite of images, my black tanka: *Fireworks*.

I had seen this drama entirely on the screen of my dreams. This vision was uniquely amenable to the instrument that awaited it. With three lights, a black cloth as decor, the greatest economy of means and enormous inner concentration, *Fireworks* was made in three days.

An example of the direct transfer of a spontaneous inspiration, this film reveals the possibilities of automatic writing on the screen, of a new language that reveals thought; it allows the triumph of the dream.

The wholly intellectual belief of the 'icy masters' of cinema in the supremacy of technique recalls, on the literary level, the analytical essays of a Poe or the methods of a Valery, who said: 'I only write to order. Poetry is an assignment.'

At the opposite pole to these creative systems there is the divine inspiration of a Rimbaud or a Lautreamont, prophets of thought. The cinema has explored the northern regions of impersonal stylisation; it should now discover the southern regions of personal lyricism; it should have its prophets.

These prophets will restore faith in a 'pure cinema' of sensual revelation. They will re-establish the primacy of the image. They will teach us the principles of their faith: that we participate before evaluating. We will give back to the dream its first state of veneration. We will recall primitive mysteries. The future of film is in the hands of the poet and his camera. Hidden away are the followers of a faith in 'pure cinema', even in this unlikely age. They make their modest 'fireworks' in secret, showing them from time to time; they pass unnoticed in the glare of the 'silver rain' of the commercial cinema. Maybe one of these sparks will liberate the cinema...

Angels exist. Nature provides 'the inexhaustible flow of visions of beauty'. It is for the poet, with his personal vision, to 'capture' them.

First published in *Cahiers du Cinéma*, no. 5, September 1951, reprinted courtesy of *Cahiers* and Kenneth Anger. Translated by David Wilson.

Kenneth Anger, 1957. Photograph by Chester Kessler.

1971

DEDICATION TO CREATE MAKE BELIEVE

Kenneth Anger interviewed by Tony Rayns

HOLLYWOOD

How important was Hollywood to you?

My relationship with Hollywood began when I was four years old, when I realised that they had let my option drop. I saw myself with a future as a child actor, and decided they had made a terrible mistake by not signing me up for a lifetime contract. I'd be a willing capitalist slave to Jack Warner to this day, if they wanted it, the way lots of artists worked for Lorenzo di Medici just for bread and butter. Fuck politics; whether they're left or right-wing is immaterial to an artist, period. The creative artist is divinely unscrupulous, and will accept any political creed that will allow him to express himself, no matter what form of subversion is necessary. We've seen this brilliantly illustrated in films this century by the 'Bolshevik' Eisenstein and the 'Nazi' Riefenstahl. Both of them were strictly only interested in themselves as creative artists.

So my relationship with Hollywood smacks of Aesop's fable of The Fox and the Grapes; over thirty years (and then some) I have developed a case of enormous, petrified, extremely sour grapes over the subject of Hollywood. There's that marvellous German word that explains the essence of the German soul - 'Schadenfreude' - that peculiarly Hunnish pleasure in seeing your enemies fall to pieces in front of your eyes. All I've had to do is sit back and wait 30 years to see the whole empire of Hollywood Babylon crumble into dust.

Naturally I had to learn sooner or later to make films with a funny little Kodak in my back yard, because they wouldn't give me a great big back lot to play with - what Orson Welles got, but he was a bigger bluff than I hope to be. ...I sent one film *Fireworks* over to the Festival des Films Maudits in Belgium, and what do I get back - not a prize, but a sweet note from Jean Cocteau, saying he thinks it's a masterpiece, coming from the dark night of the soul, which impressed me a lot at that age. So I got on the next boat and arrived at the door of the Paris Cinematheque; they showed the films and paid a little more attention...

Puce Women was my love affair with mythological Hollywood. A straight, heterosexual love affair, no bullshit, with all the great goddesses of the silent screen. They were to be filmed in their actual houses; I was, in effect, filming ghosts. When I couldn't get any bread from Freed or Kelly at MGM the project was doomed, because a freeway to the San Fernando Valley was put through all those lovely 1920 houses. That was a sad day for Hollywood, the beginning of the end, when Whitley Heights went.

I am a conservative, meaning that I cherish things of value. This places me at the antipodes of a cheap hustler like Andy Warhol, who is the garbage merchant of our time. And more power to him - he's got a lot of garbage to choose from, it's not hard. He's chosen to paint pictures that he's very proud will chip off and fall to pieces in ten years.

Anger studies Egyptian bas-relief during filming of *Lucifer Rising*.

My approach to art is the Egyptian one, and I am building for Eternity. You might as well make it in steel or carve it in the hardest granite. If it's the statue of the god or goddess you adore and it takes you twenty years to make, the chances are that an eye, a smile, a wrist, something of that figure is going to survive, maybe even when mankind is just a question mark in future archaeology.

Before I started making movies, I made puppet shows, and I'd do Chinese legends that I wrote myself - they were always Oriental. One was called *The Banana-* - that was my first script. I may still be making it, I think you're doomed to repeat yourself in that department, the first love somehow lingers.

MAGICK

Every film I've ever made has tried to impose upon the mind of the watcher an alternative reality. It's the dedication to create Make Believe.

What's the function of the Magick signs that are superimposed over the action in some of your films?

These devices are barriers to the area of the mind that I want to block out: the Cartesian frontal framework. They're keys to get frequencies through to the great Collective Unconscious, in which I totally believe (thanks to Granddaddy Jung - every sane man should believe in this one truth of the 20th Century, that we're all family on that level - or else, maybe we should just, uh, forget it.

I will blip in a 2-frame shot of a 'trademark' for the very good reason that sooner or later I want people to buy that product. I'm engaged in a long-term selling campaign. I have one product that I'm selling: the 20th Century's most misunderstood genius, called Aleister Crowley. This message has been behind my first puppet play, my first film *Who Has Been Rocking my Dream Boat*, *Fireworks*, *Puce*

Women, Pleasure Dome, Invocation of my Demon Brother and now *Lucifer Rising*. And also, incidentally, *Scorpio Rising*, which is something that happened along the way - you might call it a test pilot.

Let me give a concrete example. My line of goods is like a patent medicine show. I hold up to the audience a bottle that looks like an ordinary medicine bottle, and they have to take my word that the contents of the bottle are Magick. It does have something inside; it's transparent and looks like water, but it could be nitro-glycerine. Well, I know that I have a certain sign that I can flash, which is so simple it's like somebody scratching their head, which is a key to let's say an alchemical secret, or a golden flower, or a Venusian computer (if you want to get fancy) for changing the world.

Crowley crept into my life in the cradle, through my grandmother's fairy tales to me, which are the first things I remember. Little aphorisms - like when young Aleister asked his daddy what was that clump of stuff growing in the backyard in Leamington Spa, Daddy, in his Plymouth Brethren wisdom, said 'Don't you dare touch that, it's stinging nettles, and you'll be very sorry.' Aleister Crowley's 4-year-old answer was 'Whee!' as he leaped and spread wild in the nettle patch, where he was very happy to giggle back at Big Daddy for 72 years. Because when you join the Magickal view of the universe, you are leaping into one fucking big nettle patch for life. And I mean stinging nettles.

The metaphor of the nettle patch is that you accept the Magickal view of the universe, you are so close to out-and-out madness that if you allow your sense of concentration to waver for even a minute, you're out of the nettles and into the fiery lakes of insanity - that is the allegory of hell. The Circles of Hell is a very careful cellular analysis; this is a highly developed psychic scientist, who is dissecting the computer world of the brain and showing that there are

Anger reads a ritual by Aleister Crowley in Crowley's Temple in Cefalu, Sicily. *Thelema Abbey*

these abysses - some from which you cannot climb back, some you can risk... even if it means you get cut up and stare for eternity at your own head, mouthing back at you all the bad things you've allowed yourself to be quoted saying...

PLEASURE DOME

Why did you go back to America to make Pleasure Dome?

Because America is the Pleasure Dome of the world. Even the Chinese bitch in their blue cotton drawers for the American Pleasure Dome. The materialistic dream is so strong, that you have to be of the purity of Parsifal to banish Klingsor's castle, and tell all the flower-girls to go to hell with their own illusion. It's like what the Arabs promised their warriors in the Hashish Paradise - this is what you want, this is it, this is the feeling, nothing else but the feeling. Africa's going to buy it, Asia's going to buy it, they're going to get their two cars and colour TV set, and they're going to love it and hate it, like everybody else. They'll use up the last vestiges of the rare minerals that our crust contains, on a bunch of bullshit. Like the alchemists predicted: 'if you nourish these veins in the rocks, and pray to the gnome that protects it, he will secretly replant the garden with the crystals and minerals' - so that the Nibelungen gnomes, for instance, will rebuild the gold mines, and the silver mines. But the gnomes are being treated so shabby, it makes Uncle Walt's treatment of the Seven Dwarves seem like a beatification...

The Magician's challenge is that he declares outfront to the powers that be: 'Fuck the mystic path, I'll settle for the siddhis. ' In other words, Saint Theresa and company can go find their way right up there to the white light, but we're going to stick down here in the rainbow lightshow, because we find it a gas, and we like colour. So, you say you want to play the Magick game. This means you become a source of energy that reacts on other inert ojects in a chain

reaction, for better or worse. The Magician is sublimely indifferent to the morality of this - what you call good and evil for the Magicians of the world is just a big giggle, because it makes no difference.

So where do you want to manipulate audiences to?

I asked Aleister Crowley in a dream why he was always whispering in my ear to lead the other little kiddies up the garden path... You promise them anything at the end, but take them along, like it's an adventure and they're going to find something unexpected. The masses of the world, the people that we love, that I adore, all I want to see them do is line up with their last sheckel and drop it in the slot marked 'Kenneth Anger' and go into my Nickelodeon. I mean, it's very egotistical, but you'll have what's promised in the ad - a total experience - though it's up to you whether you come out with a blinding headache. In other words, there'll always be a penalty to pay for these artificial paradises.

KINDERGARTEN

The answer is that anything you pay your admission for is dissatisfaction, because, in the final analysis, you've been had. Say you decide one evening you're going to go out and have dinner or go to a flick - well, you should be balling your chick, very seriously, nothing else but getting yourself into the right frame of mind to make beautiful love. You see how the poor little dears are wasting their realities? Because they're letting chemicals do things for them rather than finding it in themselves and agreeing to enter once again the Great Big Kindergarten. That's why McLuhan is a great prophet - the media are going to create a new kind of mass that Marx never dreamed of; whether it's in the hands of the Chinese, the Russians, the South American military juntas, the Saudi Arabians or the German/Americans doesn't really matter: they'll all be playing these games.

Anger as the Changeling with Anita Louise as Titania in *Midsummer Night's Dream*.

Well, you are the people who wanted to be entertained. You have passed time you have sat with me for an evening. You'll never have that evening again, and it's all used up. You spent your evening away from your own reality while another reality was sitting on your head. It's like a party where you try on paper hats: some will see that it's a party (which is the whole point) and they'll fit, others will suddenly feel that they have something sitting round their head and that their nose is sticking out from under the brim, and they can't see a fucking thing. But you can't win 'em all, you really can't.

So in the time I have left, I'm grimly determined to make a feature film, in which I can lead people further up the garden path. So I can invite, in a sense, a few hundred or thousand people to my surprise party... and have it at least one evening...

First published in *Time Out*, No. 91, 1971.

PRIVATE WORLDS
by Raymond Durgnat

Kenneth Anger's *Fireworks*, made when the director was seventeen, presents dream desires with no disguise other than the aesthetic refinement indispensable for successful communication. The film is in consequence exceptionally libidinous. A youth stripped to the waist in his lonely room, leaves for adventure via a door marked 'Gents'. He finds himself in a bar, where, timidly, he approaches one of a crowd of virile sailors with a request for a light. A bunch of blazzing sticks (faggots) is drawn from a grate and thrust into his face, after which the sailors rip up his nostril, flog him with chains, splatter over his chest a milky fluid (semen?) which could seem to have spurted from his nipples like milk, and razor his breast, to find not a heart, but a chronometer-like machine, buried within the meat. A sailor lifts him up in his arms, where a low spotlight picks out his buttocks hard under the stretched jeans, as well as the sailor's flies. The image is frozen into a still photograph; the photograph burns; and the youth, with scratches on the film dancing around his head like flames, returns to 'a bed less empty than before'.

Anger has confessed his debt, for this first film, to Cocteau. The questing, half-nude poet of Cocteau's first feature is recalled by the youth stripped to the waist. Anger's mechanical heart, which only brutality can expose and uproot, recalls the ace of hearts for lack of which Cocteau's poet shoots himself in the head, to be carried off by a muscular negro. The death rite is paralleled when the matelot lifts the youth, almost tenderly, into a pose immediately frozen, preserved, and multiplied, as if by the obsessions of memory: a case, almost, of 'ennui mortel de l'immortalite' - but this youth's apotheosis is fulfilment, rather than tedium. Cocteau's tender black angel (Heurtebise, the 'collision-kiss') becomes a gang of savage white-clad matelots. The wigs, laurels and other headdresses in Cocteau's film are paralleled by the becandled, Christmas tree structure with which Anger's adolescent is crowned, as if in some transcendent convulsions of the brain - a state of inspiration, of repletion, of spiritual pregnancy imposed by the brutal yet fecund invasion of male energy. The African God which, placed in the youth's bed, erects a tent of sheet, is like a souvenir of this convulsion, a relic, fetish or icon, in the spiritually alive rather than fossilized sense of the word. The uncertain youth, undecided as to whether to seek help from maleness, to emulate maleness (asking for a light), or succumb to it in a visionary suicide, concludes as the possessor of a richly female head and an occult maleness. If the description of his bed as 'less empty than before' implies a continuation of loneliness, he has, at least, his own double sexuality, physical and spiritual, slightly exteriorized, for company.

On a first impression, the feminine seems peripheral, attained only in extremis. Yet it is more pervasive - the film's basic tension being the polarity between an inadequate and a hyperabundant maleness. The bar painted on a sheet has the flat, frail, faint, seemingly feminine quality of similar backcloths in the transvestite *Flaming Creatures*, while the towering, ornate headdress, like a regal feminization of the mind, anticipates the processional figures of Anger's next film, *Eaux d'Artifice*.

Through the Tivoli gardens, to Vivaldi's music; a Lady proceeds, in a stately, solitary 'hide and seek in a night-time labyrinth of cascades, grottoes and leaping fountains', deploying her fan like a magic wand, as if to conjure into life the sculpted male beasts among the waters and caverns, until 'the searching figure and the fountains become one'. The title is clearly a pun on feux d'artifice (fireworks), and the scratches dancing, like flames, on film, become here a labyrinth of artificial process: black-and-white photographs are hand-tinted and then printed on colour stock, through a blue filter. The feminine figure, craving the animation of masculine stone, is like an expan-

Orphee

sion of the youth's hesitant expectancy in *Fireworks*; this time the central figure's body is female while her - or his - magic command (localized in the fan) reminds one of La Princesse in *Orphee*. These frozen beasts are just how the living might appear to the dead given an only slightly altered timeslip. The blue velvet night is the antithesis of the lights offered in *Fireworks*. The processional figure, at once ultra-feminine, highly ornate and artificial, suggests a contraption rather than an organism; one thinks, waywardly perhaps, of Silvana Mangano's doll-face in the Pasolini films. Finally, however, the headdress of artifice merges with the flowing of the waters, achieves an energy complementary to that of stone. It may seem crude to suggest that the figure's progress amongst the waterfalls

and cataracts constitute a poetic equivalent of cottaging, and that the magically enlivened satyrs are the functional equivalent of the railway station youth with the tumescent crutch. But can we call in question the poetry of the one setting without equally questioning the squalor of the latter?

If *Eaux d'Artifice* is the slightest of Anger's films, it is perhaps because its key is that of a languid sensibility, a dissolution achieved by merely magic violence. Although the distinction soon shows its limitations, there is a sense in which Cocteau's world is dominated by the confrontation of male morbidity and female possessiveness, male positivity being banished to its periphery, while Anger's

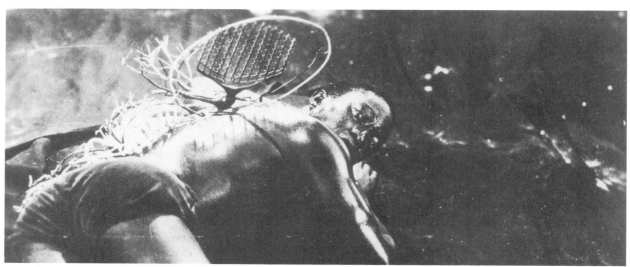

Le Sang d'un Poete

world acknowledges the female only as a demolition of or counterfeit by the male. It is clear that what on the level of overt action appear as extremes or climaxes are likely on closer inspection to reveal themselves as undercurrents running strongly and steadily throughout the action, though not yet sufficiently amassed to assert themselves. The contrast, such as it is, spreads throughout the tone and texture of their work: Cocteau's poet wends his long itinerary through 'l'hotel des folies dramatiques', the childhood theatre beyond, and by extension, the claustrophobic realism of his domestic dramas. Anger's more imperious spirit dashes all such digressions aside, as the adolescent steps directly from bed to bar. In a sense, *Fireworks* is brutal demystification of *Le Sang d'un Poete*, just as Cocteau's films explore and re-explore the zone lying between the two extremes signified by *Fireworks* (on the one side) and *Eaux d'Artifice* (on the other). Hence Cocteau's dramatic articulation and modulation are conventional and impeccable, where Anger hardly attempts

any progression which isn't violent. Cocteau's sense of balance and nuance is hospitable to realism (family dramas), and indeed to everything, whence his less enviable reputation as a touche a tout; whereas Anger's problems with dramatic structure are exemplified by his 'hotel des folies dramatiques', *Inauguration of the Pleasure Dome*, a film which went through many revisions over the years before achieving a final version bearing the subtitle: *Sacred Mushroom Edition: Lord Shiva's Dream.*

To the ritual Lord Shiva summons Astarte (Anais Nin), Hecate (Kenneth Anger), Kali, Lilith, Isis, Pan, Ganymede, and from the cinema's pantheon, the somnambulist Cesare. Shiva adopts different forms, including that of a lobster-clawed creature whom the synopsis describes as The Great Beast (reinforcing an earlier invocation of Aleister Crowley) and who might have come straight from a William Burrough's planet, or from Fellini's zone of transitional creatures, implying semi-transformations. The subtitle's reference to hallucinogenc drugs is reiterated in the quaffing of Hecate's brew, in the appearance of Ganymede, and in the envenoming of Pan's cup by Shiva. (Mythically, Ganymede was cupbearer of the Gods, associated with nectar; with soma, the Vedic moonplant, and with Aquarius (Anger's own birthsign). A merely mortal Prince, he acquired his position on Olympus by his surpassing beauty, winning over goddesses and gods alike. As mythic mortals among gods, he and Cesare doubtless represent the film-maker within his own film.)

If Shiva is Hindu God of destruction and regeneration, Pan appears in one aspect as the 'all' of created objects, and in others as a follower, or double, of Dionysus. With his poisoning the film quickens from a languid ritual to the paroxysmatic: the company bows down before Shiva in his bisexual guise, with one breast bare and two-tone lips. the pace quickens to a fivefold superimposition, through which looms the face of Kali, as if such chaos were flooding her like an orgasm-inducing energy. Stock shots of terrestrial disaster are incorporated in the action, the masked assemblage claw at the yellow-haired beauty and drag him down amidst a welter of gems, legs, boas, and lurid fingernails. The colours darken from shrill red and yellow to funereal purple, mauve and copper, to reflect the darkening and disintegration of the life-forms associated with a cosmic cycle, prior to a second cycle which would, no doubt, be the same film again.

The sybaritic panoply at this convocation of gods of orgy and disorder resumes that of the earlier films: Shiva's pyramidal headdress, insignia rings evocative of knuckledusters, Kali lighting her cigarette from a tiny horned devil while Lilith burns in red-tinted flames from *Dante's Inferno*, the association of the feminine with liquid as the women proffer bowls of nectar to the men. A contrast is provided by an urn-vase from which a red liquid, nearer the consistency of Technicolor blood than of wine, is poured into goblets. Their rims are shaped like lotus blossoms, their stems recall candles and they import an implicit obscenity to the act of sipping. A sado-masochistic bisexuality is re-echoed in the dominance of Kali, a carroty-haired drag queen upreared as haughtily as She. The three-winged mirror of narcissism-in-the-round is prominent. Bunches of grapes dangling from a male belt become incitations to recumbent fellatio, while red-pink boots, like satyr hoofs, tread firmly on flowered carpets, whose effect of artificialized nature evokes Symbolism.

Visually at least the film sports a heavily ornamented surface reminiscent at times of its near-contemporary, Michael Powell's *Tales of Hoffman* (the plethora of strange-hued fingernails and the fishnet-stockinged feet in fur recall Ludmilla Tcherina's red-nailed feet dancing over

Tales of Hoffman

31

Tales of Hoffman

the petrified torsos of her male victims). Anger's shot of Cesare in black gliding past yellow candles anticipates Corman's Poe, whose aesthetic is also associated with a narcissistic, magic and sado-masochistic thematic. Once again, pulp fiction and the avant-garde ally themselves as a perpetuation of the Romantic and Symbolist traditions.

Anger's plot, likewise, is heavily encrusted, not so much with ornamentation, as with tautology, given the similari-ties between the various gods and the problems of devel-oping relationships between divinities, who, since they incarnate primal forces, scarcely lend themselves to the inner divisons and outward adaptations on which drama depends. The poisoning of Pan by Shiva and the primal chaos which ensues parallel the destruction of The Dreamer by the sailors and his subsequent charging with spiritual electricity. The essential interplay is between a lesser force and a greater, which, being greater, must destroy as it enriches. In neo-Platonist terms, Shiva is idea, Pan is matter; both, however, are amoral, and the style of their incarnations must appear as evil to a Christianized sensibility: it is as if Anger were to Neo-Platonism as Sade to Christianity. Evil, not good, is ultimate, at least in the sense in which energy, being amoral, is only accidentally good, and in its wilfulness, essentially evil. The polarity between good and evil is replaced by that between activity and passivity, yet the necessity of the victim's role expels winner-loser Manicheanism while requiring cruelty in a more Dionysiac form. The ambivalence of drink (nectar, drug, and venom) recalls the close association of blood and milk, as joint products of torture, in *Fireworks*, and in Cocteau, snowball and poison-ball; while the insidious hints of fellatio suggest a substitution of phallus for breast. The associated theme of the destruction of the breast appears in the crustacean claw, as in the razor of *Fireworks*, and even, perhaps, in the ornamentation of the goblets whose leaflike rims are a queasy compromise between a vegetable limpness and barbs and thorns. Such associations clarify the focus on cigarette lighting and flames in three of the four Anger films; fire as phallic energy between the lips, besought or brutally imposed; just as the necklace 'drunk' by a reclining God in red silk is an equivocation between the feminine (a woman's ornament, loop, the round liquid forms) and the not quite masculine (both gravity and teeth make of the loop a limp column).

The tonus of violence in Cocteau is different, emphasizing a kind of strangulation or suffocation (like a climax of claustrophobia). The welling of blood from the corner of a mouth or a nostril, which suggests at once vagina and nipple, is common to both directors. In general, violence in Cocteau is primarily emotional and familial, and physicalized only in climax. In Anger, the drama is residual, and symbol and violence reign.

Anger's film is laden so heavily with magic as almost to paralyse itself. Its monumentality becomes inertia, albeit an aesthetically beautiful, because measured, one; its bisexuality a splendid apathy rather than a tension. Minor interplay apart, the gods, until the poisoning, seem isolated and enclosed in narcissistic *esse*, from which they are released into a chaotic, transpersonal, transparent 'confusion and running together'. Throughout, oppressively rich hues are enhanced by their degradation in shadow.

Scorpio Rising returns to the male brotherhood of *Fireworks*. The youth and the matelot gang have merged into a motorcycle club. The adolescent yearning is accompanied by a mellow, ironic author's-third-person which deepens rather than adulterates the saturnine sense of powers at play. The uninitiated spectator might see merely a suspiciously fascinated warning of a rising tide of anomie and violence about to engulf America. But Anger speaks of a 'high view of the Myth of the American motorcyclist', and 'high' relates, one suspects, to magic rather than to hallucinogens or a lofty philosophical perspective. Any problem of dramatic articulation is solved by a division into sections, with an initally enervated rhythm slowly quickening throughout. 'The machine as tribal totem, from toy to terror. Thanatos in chrome and black leather.' The force concentrated in the *Fireworks* dreams or in the Symbolist universe of metaphysical ritual now inspires a real existence, yet the realistic details retain a ritual weight. These naive yet profoundly attuned youths correspond to Pan, with machine speed and Fascist violence corresponding to the envenomed drink which restores fossilized energies, shedding mere identities to achieve their Heraclitean blur of speed. In *Fireworks*, the camera is identified with the Dreamer; in *Scorpio Rising* it looks on, giving the film its feeling of being, sometimes a documentary, sometimes an apprehension of occult correspondences and connections, beamed, seductively, on the spectator, and offering the Cerberus of his commonsense a sop only to breach his emotional defences. More than any previous Anger films, *Scorpio Rising* parades its seductive joy, anticipating and surpassing the best of Arrabal.

Anger's own synopsis divides the film into four parts. 'Part I: Boys and Bolts (masculine fascination with the Thing that Goes)' begins with a tiny toy of a police motorcyclist and moves into a sequence worshipping the machine-fetish in the garage where its acolyte tends it. In blue-toned shots evoking the nocturnal zone of *Eaux d'Artifice*, light strikes silver stars from its chrome. Masculine in its metal and energy, the machine is imbued with a female, or rather a pederastic docility as a girls' pop group sings 'Wind me up'. The camera drifts over and about the machine, whose petrol tank is imbued with a

Anger in a production still.

queasily spongy tactility, and comes to rest on a configuration of exhaust pipe outlet, boots and chain. Their fetishized violence insidiously recalls the sting in the tail of the animal whose name the film bears, as well as, by their position, overtones of anal outrage. Like a death-barge,

the machine awaits, seductively, its victim-rider (one thinks of the white steed in *La Belle et la Bete*). The presence of a feminine death-widow figure seems quite superfluous, an unnecessary aesthetic imposition. A sumptuously muscled male abdomen is eased and buckled into denim and leather, while Bobby Vinton sings 'She wore blue velvet; bluer than velvet was the night; softer than satin was the light...' Fetishism invests the person whose every gesture and act now becomes sacramental - even if, like the Cissy Cyclist who winces as he strikes a match on his teeth, not all believers are worthy of their belief.

From blue as dominant to gold for 'Part II: Image Maker (Getting High On Heroes)'. A cyclist lies on his bed, with yellow-blond hair, probaby dyed, iodine-tinted glasses, and a marmalade cat; the tonality brings out every yellow patch in close-up inserts of the comic strip which he is perusing. Making the most of Dogpatch innocence, two Al Capp youths strike up a Tom-and-Huck friendship which the new context renders distinctly equivocal. With the rock songs used throughout the film, and Brando in *The Wild One* on the television set, implications of an unconscious but insistent perversity are set reverberating throughout a whole culture - while being, perhaps less obtrusively, implicit in the structure of human sexuality and society, whatever its particular forms. Rising, the youth caparisions himself for a ride, his preparations climaxing with a sniff of cocaine from a bottle theatrically labelled 'Poison'. His sneeze is marked with a quick insert in a contrasting colour.

The lifestyle moves towards one of the cimaxes which are its raison d'etre: 'Part III: Walpurgis Night (Cyclers' Sabbath)'. *The Wild One* gives place to a Biblical film whose amateurishness betrays all that is prim and shrewish in mediocre piety, in its hopeless negating of energy (not for nothing are we reminded of Jesus-Sade's carton-paste castle at the end of *L'Age d'Or*). As disciples in cottonwool beards file through a flimsy Palestine, cyclists enter the gang hut, leaping about in party dress, including hilariously lumpy drag and a skeleton suit garnished with rubber phallus. The party, like Christianity, has its sacrifice: Kris Jensen sings the stealthily voluptuous 'Torture' as the victim's mates sit on him, smearing mustard on his lower abdomen. Jesus looks disgustedly at something in that direction while a disciple handles two money-bags, evoking the victim's testicles, while faintly un-complaisant screams irrupt on the soundtrack. Jesus seems unable to get his Palm Sunday ass started while the cyclists roar off. A red-wigged skull (recalling the carroty-haired Kali at Shiva's ceremony) has a fag marked 'Youth' between its lips (as Shiva condemns Pan). In the two eye-sockets, like the portholes of a fruit machine, appear two panels of Christ urging a clean-limbed boy along some righteous path, snickers are heard on the soundtrack.

'Part IV: Rebel Rouser (A Message From Our Sponsor)', our sponsor being, no doubt, our inspirer, Lucifer. The orgy becomes a pre-apocalyptic reign of terror, a lumpenproletarian, male version of *Rosemary's Baby*. Before a Gothic arch which establishes the location as a church, a motocyclist standing on high in SS cap and mask, harangues and exhorts, scattering hymnbooks and waving a torch. His sermon is intercut with weaker, paler images of a cyclists' rally, while the black priest's gesticulations recall the semaphore with the chequered flag. Cycling now has taken second place, has surrendered its energy, to a diabolism which becomes something like a black mass when a cyclist in the church turns his back on us, relieves himself into his helmet, and offers it to the congregation and us, as if it were the consecrated wine. The atmosphere of Nazi revivalism includes a brief, almost indecipherable, close-up of what appears to be a discipline helmet, i.e. a black leather hood, padded with foam rubber, used to blind, gag, and voluptuously incarcerate the victim in sado-masochistic punishment games. In the rally there is a slew, a skid, a crash; the red light atop of a police car revolves like a Janus-faced divinity of life and death, rhythmically cut in and out of close-up, so as to pulsate, like a regular tolling of a bell. The circle has been completed, from police department as toy to police department as aloof system. In almost the opening shot, a cyclist's bullet-head rears up from the lower edge of the frame; later, a cyclist's donning of his headgear is emphasized by meticulous cutting; the theme of head and eyes is resumed by the fruit-machine skull, the SS half-mask and the bondage-hood, and climaxed by the flashing, revolving red light, like an all-seeing eye, an incandescent mind, a head of pure blood and light.

In a variety of ways Anger's aesthetic recalls Eisenstein's. The intensive use of montage in the strict intellectual sense, as also of details which, whether within or without the immediate scenic context, are organized into symbolic digressions (like Kerensky's statuettes in *October*). Both directors respond to mystic regalis (the tending of the motorcycle corresponding to the opening coronation in

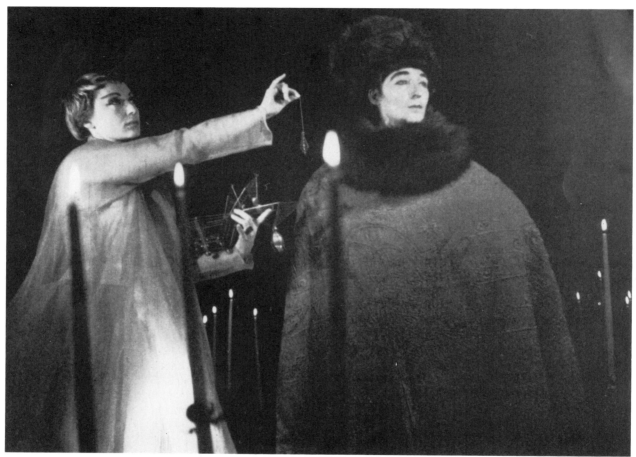

Inauguration of the Pleasure Dome

Ivan the Terrible - a somewhat 'Scorpionic' film), while their styles involve a curious compound of abstruseness and over-emphasis. *Scorpio Rising* is primarily a structure of ideas and only secondarily a narrative; it is paradoxically essential to its purpose that the images of riding be few and weak, and any sense of speed and exhilaration conspicu- ously absent. The cult of energy threatens us all, but only the death of the cultist is interesting. The scorpion rises, only to kill itself. Sadism is nine-tenths masochism. Yet masochistic death is equally illumination, the cosmic cycle sustained.

ELUSIVE LUCIFER
by Tony Rayns

No other contemporary film-maker has fuelled his own mythology as much as Kenneth Anger. He zealously protects his real name even from close associates; he gives interviewers substantially different accounts of his life and work; and he continually revises his own films, sometimes radically altering their meaning by changing the entire soundtrack. These notes are an attempt to construct an accurate outline of his career since 1966 and, in particular, to cut through some of the confusion surrounding the different versions of *Lucifer Rising*.

Anger moved from New York (where he had made *Scorpio Rising*) to the West Coast in late 1964 or early 1965. He set out to make a kind of scientific extension of *Scorpio* about California's hot-rod drivers and their lovingly customised cars, and apparently shot nearly thirty minutes of usable material for it, but edited only the three-minute fragment *Kustom Kar Kommandos*. (His outline for the full project is reprinted in P. Adams Sitney's *Visionary Film*, 1974). This was released in 1965, as 'work in progress'. In fact, though, Anger abandoned the project; he evidently lost interest in it as he became fascinated with the first stirrings of Californian 'psychedelia'. In 1966, he edited the 'Sacred Mushhroom Edition' of *Inauguration of the Pleasure Dome*, using up to five layers of superimposition in the images and Janacek's *Glagolitic Mass* as the soundtrack.

By this time he was living in San Francisco in the mansion known as the 'Russian Embassy' at 1198 Fulton Street. The Lucifer project began to take shape towards the end of 1966. Sheldon Renan's book *An Introduction to the American Underground Film* (1967) reported that the film was a to be about the 'holy' war between the outgoing Piscean Age and the incoming Aquarian Age, as seen in the conflict between teenagers and their parents; one scene was planned to show hippies kneeling along the San Andreas Fault, praying for a 'liberating earthquake'. Anger confirmed this general impression in an interview he gave to Jonathan Cott (*The Sunday Ramparts*, April 1967): *It's a film about the Love Generation, but seen in depth - like the Fourth Dimension. It's about love - the violence as well as the tenderness....There's an invisible war going on. It's of Miltonic proportions and it's a war between the forces of life and death, love and hate. The film* Lucifer Rising *is a prophecy. I see the embodiment of love among the children as winning. Lucifer is actually a sunshine child - Little Sunshine....* San Francisco artist Rick Griffin produced a Dore-esque poster for the film with the slogan - 'a love vision'.

Anger told several interviewers (notably Mick Brown in *Crawdaddy*, 1976) that his first Lucifer was a remarkable five-year old named Godot, who fell to his death from a window, posssibly believing he could fly. He also told both Cott and Brown about a mysterious encounter with a mental hospital escapee: he performed Aleister Crowley's 'Invocation of the Bornless One' in Golden Gate Park at dawn and was rewarded with the appearance of a young man who called himself 'Joe Lucifer', described himself as a 'a man in a woman's orbit', and slipped away from Anger's home a few days later, leaving only his boots behind him, before Anger had a chance to film him. This fleeting visitor apparently gave him valuable guidance for the project. Anger's next 'Lucifer' was the nineteen year old Robert K. Beausoleil, who moved into the house on Fulton Street. According to Ed Sanders (*The Family*, 1971), Anger formed a band called the Magick Powerhouse of Oz to perform the music for the film, with Beausoleil as its lead guitarist and sitarist.

There is an extremely interesting account of Anger, Beausoleil and their circle in Roger Peyrefitte's 'factual novel', *Les Americains* (1968). Although Peyrefitte is somewhat preoccupied with the intricacies of anti-homosexual legislation in various of the United States, his report of his conversations with Anger includes some details of *Le Lever de Lucifer*, asides on Kinsey, hippies and California's many groups of occultists, and a vivid account of an orgiastic love-in at a Methodist church on Ellis Street, where Beausoleil's band performed naked.

On September 21, 1967, Anger organised a celebration of the Equinox of the Gods at the Straight Theatre on Haight Street. The band played, Anger conducted magick rituals and the proceedings were filmed. The event may have been a benefit to raise money for the completion of the film. Either during or soon after that evening, some sixteen hundred feet of edited rushes for *Lucifer Rising* were stolen, along with some equipment and Anger's car. *Lucifer* had been shot on reversal stock and there was no negative of the missing footage. Anger has no doubt that Beausoleil was the thief. In any event, Beausoleil disappeared at the same time as the film. He was soon associated with Charles Manson, and arrested for the murder of the music teacher Gary Hinman; he is currently serving a life sentence in Tracy Prison.

In mid-October, Anger went to the office of the Film-makers Co-op in New York, and there burned what he said were his unreleased films in front of Jonas Mekas and others. He went on to buy a full black-bordered page in the Village Voice (October 26 issue) to announce his 'death': *In Memoriam - Kenneth Anger - Film-maker 1947-1967*. He then proceded to Washington to take part in one of the largest anti-Vietnam protests, the March on the Pentagon. Anger reappeared in London in 1968. Far from abandoning film-making, he entered a highly productive phase. He edited *Rabbit's Moon* from the rushes of his *La Lune des Lapins*, shot in Paris in the early 1950's and stored in the Cinematheque Francaise ever since. He reissued his 1948 short *Puce Moment* with a new soundtrack. And he set about editing the few remaining fragments of *Lucifer Rising*. After at least three 'trial' versions, he released the eleven-minute *Invocation of My Demon Brother*, with a synthesiser track by Mick Jagger. The film incorporated a small amount of new footage (notably of the Rolling Stones' 1969 Hyde Park concert), but principally drew upon the footage shot at the Equinox of the Gods event in

September 1967. Anger called the film 'the last blast of Haight consciousness'.

Anger's British distributor at the time was Jimmy Vaughn, of Vaughn-Rogosin Films, whose chief business was selling American avant-garde films to German TV. Anger, living in the basement apartment of Vaughn's house in Hampstead, began to formulate plans for a new *Lucifer Rising*. He told the diarist of *The Times* (July 11, 1969) about

Lucifer Rising

San Francisco artist Rick Griffin's poster for *Lucifer Rising*.

an Aleister Crowley project that would 'intersperse Crowley's spiritual life with contemporary events, such as the sinking of the Titanic'), and mentioned Nicol Williamson as a possible choice to play the young Crowley. Soon after, he discovered a new Lucifer in the person of young Middlesbrough steel-worker Leslie Huggins, and brought him to London. Vaughn pre-sold *Lucifer Rising* to the German TV station NDR, and Anger began shooting with Huggins in 1970, using his Hampstead apartment as a 'studio'. Before long, he moved to a considerably larger apartment in Mount Street, Mayfair. Huggins proved to be no less elusive than previous Lucifers, and schedules were more than once interrupted by the actor's disappearances. During one such hiatus, Anger edited the eight-minute *Lucifer Rising: Chapter One* (1971), using the Hampstead rushes; this centred on the Magus' dance around the magick circle to invoke Lucifer, and ended like an episode of a serial. Then the National Film Finance Corporation was persuaded to invest in *Lucifer Rising*, prompting the outraged headline 'Devil Film to get State Aid' in *The Sunday Telegraph* (March 28, 1971). The additional funding enabled Anger to shoot on locations in Egypt and Germany (the Celtic rock-temple in the Lilith scenes). Back in London, Anger used his Mount Street apartment as a 'studio' for further interiors and for such 'special effects' as the glass shot of the Adept 'at' Stonehenge. It was at this point that the film theorist Noel Burch briefly worked on the film.

Shooting halted when Anger broke with Jimmy Vaughn, who had been increasingly pre-occupied with more commercial ventures. Anger moved to New York with his rushes, and in 1973 edited a twenty-five minute version of *Lucifer Rising*, with music by Jimmy Page. This was broadly similar to the present version, but lacked the shots of volcanic eruptions, many of the special visual effects, and all the shots featuring the character of the Adept. Vaughn's company meanwhile went in to receivership. In 1975, Anger published the first English language edition of his book *Hollywood Babylon*, and toured the US with a special film presentation to promote it. In 1976, he returned to London, to extricate the *Lucifer Rising* negatives from the receiver; while there, he publicly 'fired' Jimmy Page from his work on the soundtrack. Back in New York, he prepared yet another version of *Inauguration of the Pleasure Dome* (1978), this time with an Electric Light Orchestra soundtrack, and a seven-minute version of *Rabbit's Moon* (1979). He then resumed work on *Lucifer*, with the aid of a grant from the National Endowment for the Arts, and released the present version in 1981. It carries original music by Bobby Beausoleil (interviewed by Truman Capote in the recent collection *Music for Chameleons*), with whom Anger has been corresponding ever since his imprisonment.

Reprinted by courtesy of Monthly Film Bulletin; this article was first published in MFB, September 1982.

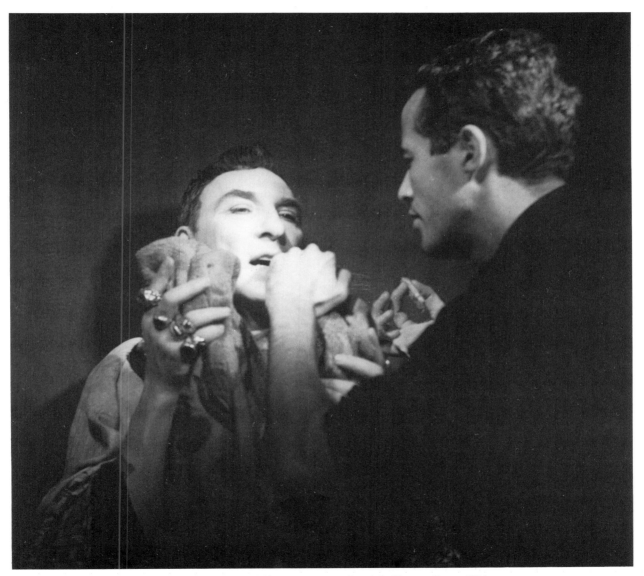

Anger applies make-up to Samson De Brier as Lord Shiva in *Inauguration of the Pleasure Dome*, 1954.

1989

FLAMES IN THE NIGHT

Kenneth Anger interviewed by Rebekah Wood

You're back in Hollywood again. Is that home?

I really feel like a gypsy. I don't identify. I suppose it is. Certainly I was born here, but I can feel at home in Paris or London. This is a funny place. I've come back hoping perhaps to make a commercial movie. It's a big 'perhaps'.

Your apartment houses your collection of Hollywood memorabilia. Have you been saving things for long?

Yes. I began at five, when my grandmother gave me some buttons which belonged to Rudolph Valentino. My collection has mostly been in storage in the attics and basements of friends' houses and it's only recently that I've been able to gather everything together. I have about half of it here.

I notice you can collect Kenneth Anger films on video now.

A test was made and they look good on video. The fact is many more people are able to purchase them than have ever been able to collect 16mm prints of my films. It isn't the same as seeing them on a screen. That's how I prefer

them to be seen, but I accept it and I also gladly accept an additional way to increase my revenue. I don't exist in an ivory tower like some gay nineties aesthete. I'm not panicking , but I have to think about that. 'Nothing gets easier', as Bette Davis once said about growing old.

It is very sealed from the outside world in here.

Well, I hope so, while the outside is the physical town - Hollywood. Hollywood is not what it used to be - where is? It's become in many ways a third world shanty-town; of course the stars live in Bel-Air and Malibu.

Starting at the beginning: A Midsummer Night's Dream - that fantasy film world - do you think it turned a boy's head to be doing something like that, at four?

No. It was made very clear to me I was going to have a tiny part in one film, there was never any question about becoming a child actor as a career.

You didn't want to?

Yes. But my parents didn't want me to. It was a curious little experience. I got the part because my grandmother knew Max Rheinhardt, but also I had been going to the Theodore Kosloff dancing school, so, I could follow directions - a certain amount of pantomime and prancing about - no talk. It was awesome and certainly marked me. I mean it was dazzling.

Mickey Rooney played Puck.

He was twelve and I was four, but oddly enough he was friendly. He noticed me. He took me on a little tour of the studios and when we came to the prop department there were sixty neon violins left over from *Gold Diggers* of *1933*.

Kenneth Anger 'at home' with his collection of Hollywood memorabilia.

The prop man said, 'You can't have one. You'll just break it.' I said 'No. I'll look after it for ever. I will be very careful.' I've still got that neon violin, it works - it glows. It's presently on exhibit at the Museum of Moving Image in London.

When you were a child, you were making movies.

Well, I decided I wanted to make films, but on my own. I must have been seven. Our family had a 16mm wind-up Kodak cinecamera which was used on holidays, birthday parties, the usual home-movie type of thing. One year, after we'd all had a trip to Yosemite, there were a few spools of unexposed film left over and I said, 'These are going to expire; let me use them up.' So I was given permission to do that.

But your family didn't continue to encourage your cinematic enterprises?

They let me use the camera. That was already something. And I didn't break it. I was very careful. So, it developed as a kind of hobby, even though I never looked on it as any kind of a lark. I took myself quite seriously as a child. I was going to make films and put my name on them: 'A film by Kenneth Anger'.

Fireworks must have upset your parents a bit.

They never saw it, so they couldn't be upset. It was made when they were out of town. The places where it was shown were not where they were. *Fireworks* was shown very little in the forties - one or two showings, at Cinema 16 in New York and at the San Francisco Museum. In other words, it was treated as an underground film, which is what it was, semi-clandestine and subversive.

Anger with Anita Louise in *A Midsummer Night's Dream*.

Your grandmother helped with Fireworks?

Bertha saw it. She thought it was 'terrific' but she was the maverick of the family. She was just a character, you know, independent-minded. She didn't discourage me from being an artist, quite the opposite. The fact I had chosen an impractical career didn't faze her. She was a painter herself. I'm afraid my father wanted me to be an aeronautical engineer like him, at Douglas Aircraft - I didn't feel I was cut out for that.

What's the particular appeal for you of Valentino as a star?

I like the stars of the silent era, there's something about the lack of a voice that makes the character of the star more mythic... and to me he had fabulous charisma. Now, he wasn't the only silent star that had sexual charisma, but he was the first one... the one that was a love-object, a boudoir boy, let's put it that way. He more than any other, was like a total turn on to me.

Fireworks *was made in 1947. That's the year that Aleister Crowley died... coincidence.? I mean were you aware of that?*

I knew about Crowley, but only just. I'd read some of his books. I knew his magical son Jack Parsons. But I didn't get to Europe until 1950.

The opening shot in Fireworks, *the dreamer in the arms of the sailor, reminds me of Fay Wray and King Kong.*

It's that kind of thing, of a beast, of the protagonist being carried away by a brute. I don't think I was consciously imitating, but certainly some of my inspiration comes from things I've observed in life; in movies, in paintings, or things I dream about. Inspiration comes from many sources.

I see you're attributed with various nationalities and birth-dates; and you changed your name. That's a very Hollywood thing to do.

Well, that's ALL WRONG, because I haven't changed my name. Various things have been written about me which are wrong - dead wrong! I was born in 1930, and the family name is Anger, which is German for a 'meadow' or 'field'. If you look in the Berlin phone book there are pages of Angers. We Angers are a good Kraut bunch from way back.

After Fireworks *your next project was* Puce Women.

It ended up being a moment, but it was supposed to be a feature film and it used a series of stunning women denoting various times of day. There was to be Miss dawn, Miss morning, Lady noon, Dame afternoon, and Dowager evening, and so the fragment was one little bit of it, which I called *Puce Moment*.

Why Puce?

Puce is a colour, the changeable colour of a flea, and puce is the colour of her sequined gown. It was the name of a purple-green iridescent colour that was very popular in the 1920's - puce and tango were jazz age colours

OK. That's the first of your movies not completed as orginally planned, something that has been a pattern in your career. You've consistently over-reached yourself. You've been an incredibly ambitious film-maker.

And an inept producer of my own projects. I don't think I was overly ambitious, but the practical thing of finding enough money, or of not running out of money is something I've run up against a number of times: money doesn't come easily - say, by a relative dying and leaving me something. And then I end up with less than I'd hoped for, so I will eventually make a shorter film, rather than just chucking it all.

Making films - the kind you've made, looking for things which go beyond the outer mechanics of action and events ... the invisible factor - that must take real clarity of purpose.

I have a pretty clear idea of what the film will be like before I begin and all the main things I want to include in it. I try to take just the scenes I need. Not endless re-takes. I've had to pre-cut them in my mind. I've also done the obvious thing: when I've had more money, I've done a few more takes, three or four is a luxury. I still work very tight.

You're a self-declared explorer of sexuality, but your movies aren't sexually graphic.

My concept of sensuality and eroticism is through suggestion and inference To me a shadow is always much more evocative and intriguing than anything explicit. It's a little bit what Marlene Dietrich said: 'Desire is everything, having is nothing.' It's the longing - the desire - not the nuts and bolts.

After your early period in Hollywood, you went to Paris, encouraged by Cocteau.

Yeah, I got a fan letter from Cocteau. He'd seen my film *Fireworks* at the Biarritz 'Festival du Film Maudit'. He was on the jury and I rather think he was responsible for the film being awarded a prize.

Did you speak French then?

I certainly did 'cos I majored in French at Beverly Hills High School. I've always been fascinated by French culture, and my grandmother encouraged me to study it. Then just imagine riding in a taxi up the Champs Elysees with all those names on the marquees - Cocteau, Piaf.

You must have felt quite adventurous - hopeful - setting off to Paris.

Oh yeah. I was looking forward... to jump into Europe. It was something! I arrived in spring, 1950. At that time, Cocteau's movies were playing - *Les Parents Terribles*, *Les Enfants Terribles*. It was a pretty exciting time. I got to meet Colette, Chanel, Piaf, Genet, Cocteau, Henri Langlois, all in one fell swoop.

Un Chant d'Amour is often shown with or paralleled to Fireworks.

I met Genet and he just shrugged his own movie off. The film was paid for by the owner of the Rose Rouge nightclub, Nico Papadakis, and so it had more production values. It was filmed on 35mm with a professional cameraman, so it certainly had a more slick look than my little film - but I think I did pretty good, with my hundred dollar budget.

What about Cocteau?

Of all his films, the one I felt a most direct relation to is *Le Sang du Poete*. I think it's a very impressive piece of work. He's certainly one of the artists I most admire, along with Noel Coward. They're both one-man bands, one-man shows and I always wanted to do that, to do it all myself. I've been that way since I was a kid. When I was very young, I had my own puppet-show. I worked all the puppets myself. You know, when there's six of seven

Le Sang d'un Poete

marionettes on stage, that's rather something. But I figured a way to do it all myself.

But Noel Coward - he was pretty establishment wasn't he?

No. No. No. When he started he was writing dirty plays about drugs and incest. Both Coward and Cocteau made avant-garde plays. Coward's play *The Vortex*, that was his shocker. He was something like twenty when he did that. He acted in it, playing the drug-addict. He wrote it and then he got into writing music. I've always wanted to do that. I love music. Wish I could write my own.

Your first film in Paris was Rabbit's Moon.

La Lune des Lapins came about through a series of fortuitous events. A Russian film company had a number of

spools of 35mm stock left over from a documentary they were making. It was good fine-grain black and white. The idea of having 35mm to work with, even though it was only a few thousand feet, was terrific. The second thing was that Pierre Braunberger had a small studio behind the Pantheon. He offered it to me for the month of August. I almost finished it, but then he came back and said I had to vacate the place, so I had to tear down and get out. I only had two weeks there, but what I did manage to film, I eventually cut into *Rabbit's Moon*.

Rabbit's Moon *is a very directly emotional film.*

It's what I call a nocturne, a dream about me. It's about unrequited love and the moon is a symbol, as it has been in romantic literature (at least up to Apollo) of the unattainable. The moon has always been something that's longed for. I use the figures of Commedia: Pierrot, the lost

Claude Revenant as Harlequin in *Rabbit's Moon.*

clown; Columbine, the flirt; and Harlequin, who's the devil, the trickster.

Your Harlequin is very spiteful.

So he is. The world, to Harlequin, is a comedy. To him, it's uproarious to trick - to trip people up. Harlequin is Lucifer. To look at it from Harlequin's standpoint - which may be the devil's point of view - he's having a good time. In other words, Harlequin has no complexes; his approach to the world is very direct. You can call him cruel, but he is also a survivor and Pierrot the sad sack is not.

It was six years between Fireworks *and the next finished film* Eaux d'Artifice. *That must have been discouraging.*

It was very discouraging. I was having my alchemical experiments blow-up, rather than produce the mythic gold. So, when I went to Italy and was able to make *Eaux d'Artifice,* it was gratifying to be able to finish the film as I had originally intended. *Eaux D'Artifice* is another nocturne - a film about myself searching in the moonlight - or looking for something to happen in the dark.

After that, you made Inauguration of the Pleasure Dome *here, in California.*

Yes. I came back from Europe. My mother died and I made the film with all of the money she left me. I also had a terrific group of friends who helped me to make the film: the poetess Anais Nin, and the diarist Samson de Brier with his house full of all kinds of exotica.

You've featured some odd characters in that film: Osirus, Shiva Cagliostro...

48

Anger and Dr. Alfred C. Kinsey explore the ruins of Aleister Crowley's Temple in Cefalu, Sicily. *Thelema Abbey*, 1955.

Cagliostro was a magician, a character who was possibly a fake and possibly the real thing, and that always intrigues me.

And there's the mystic painter Cameron...

She was the widow of my friend Jack Parsons who had died while I was away in Europe. His house was blown-up in a mysterious accident that may have been an alchemical accident or a murder plot by Howard Hughes... but Jack knew how to handle explosives, because he invented the jet fuel that took the rocket to the moon - so its unlikely he'd drop a bottle of nitroglycerine.

Your work, your concerns , are very engaged with Crowley. Why no film about 'the Beast'?

I have made one documentary, *Thelema Abbey* on Crowley's erotic frescos. That film was made for an extinct British magazine *Picture Post*, TV Omnibus. and they lost it. It's untraceable. I'd dearly like to film some of Crowley's rituals, possibly some episodes from his life which were lurid and over the top and would lend themselves to film and have comedy and tragedy and roisterous adventure. I certainly know my subject - well as anyone ever can. Though I never met the wickedest man in the world as Beaverbrook labeled him.

You'd spent over ten year s in France. When you came back to live in New York you must have felt like a stranger.

It's always been strange to me there anyway. Brooklyn was as strange to me as any foreign country. I was invited to stay with friends in Brooklyn, by another film-maker, Marie Menken. When I was there I went out to Coney Island and met this group of bikers, who had built themselves showbikes, very flamboyant machines - dozens of headlights, chrome fins and things, basically made to show off. That was the origin of *Scorpio Rising*.

Scorpio's the sign that governs death and sexuality...

....and machines. So there is a direct connection with motocycles, weapons, the mechanical aspect of things.

That teen-dream, the rebel-biker mythos, it's been imitated a lot.

Yes, I was the first one to use pop music. Sometimes I'm called the godfather of MTV (laughs). I made my music track out of songs of that summer, songs that were just around. It sort of identified that summer. I didn't steal them, I paid the rights: fifteen thousand dollars - cost a lot more now. I think I was the first to use pop music as ironic commentary on the image, in the way that I did.

Was Scorpio Rising *in some sense a commercial venture on your part?*

No, it was just the subject. No, it's one of my films that's had more recognition, but it's a 'short'. It got some publicity - praise and prizes - it was banned in Los Angeles and it was a landmark case when the Californian Supreme Court said it could be shown...it had 'redeeming merit.'

Then you went straight on to begin Kustom Kar Kommandos, *working with a very new colour range.*

Oh, yeah. In that respect, it was to be completely different from *Scorpio Rising*.. It was to be, for one thing, very Californian, lots of bright pastels. *Scorpio Rising* was more like the flames in the night, darkness, mystery. This was to be far more optimistic. But the protagonist, who was to be a little bit the equivalent of the main character in *Scorpio Rising* (in other words, I would follow through one character), unfortunately he was killed in a drag-race and I allowed this to discourage me from continuing.

Invocation of My Demon Brother *came next. The demon brother/lover, that's something I associate with you. Can you tell me something about what this means?*

It's the eidolon, or the secret double who is possibly a demon and possibly an angel. It's either your better self or your worse self, or the part of you that's needed to become complete. In my own life, it goes back to my childhood, where I had an invisible playmate who may or may not have had more reality than imagination. It was real for me. His name was Jackie, so the demon brother does appear.

You articulate yourself as Magus - that's how you show yourself. It's very magical to watch, but it's serious; it's an important feature isn't it?

I have studied ritual magic. It's my avocation. It's actually more than study. I would like to be a Magus. In a film, there can be a certain amount of will-fulfilment, seriously, the magus should perform alone, not surrounded by technicians, lights and a camera. I made myself the robe of the magus and I drew the magic circle and I perform an invocation. However, in some alarming ways, it became true. In some ways, it was like playing at something and having it become very real. When I met Bobby Beausoleil, he fulfilled, in many ways, the role of this demon in real life. Suddenly I was confronted with the very flesh and blood - a handsome Devil.

So Invocation of My Demon Brother *is orginal* Lucifer Rising *footage?*

It's all I had left after Bobby stole all he could find... well, he overlooked some unspooled scraps in the cutting-bin, and from these, I constructed *Invocation of My Demon Brother*.

It's got footage of Vietnam..

When I put the film together, Vietnam was very much on my mind. It was happening. The helicopters and the troops jumping out - that was an image I wanted in the film as an underlying background of violence and chaos.

I don't associate you with being politically engaged...

You may not, but there are certain things. Certainly I was opposed to the Vietnam war - vainglorious, foolish and tragic. There are causes that I am very much concerned with, like the environment, and I'm not too fond of nuclear power. That's an example of arrogance: power that produces garbage that's lethal for thousands of years.

A lot of focus is put on that period as a time of personal and public crisis in your career. What about the obituary you took out in 'Village Voice'?

It looked like an obituary, but to anyone that know me...it wasn't, because the dates on it corresponded with my years of film-making. I was upset to have my feature-film stolen. I preferred to ... I needed to publicly exorcise it, otherwise it would have eaten away at me. I got it out of my system in that way.

After that, you spent some time in England.

Yes, England was a refuge for me in the late 60's and early 70's, and I did the cutting for *Invocation of My Demon Brother*. I also cut *Rabbit's Moon* which had been misplaced by the Cinematheque Francaise, lost for twenty years - and they refound it at that time. So I was happy to dig into that and do a bit of personal archaeology. In England, I found backing from the National Film Finance Corporation and

I began to film *Lucifer Rising* again, but this time with a completely different take on it.

It seems to me a very different kind of film. It looks radically different.

I hope so. I want every film to be an exploration into new territory. I came to the realization that there's things that I love about the world that I hadn't yet got up on the screen and I'd better start doing that, so there's more nature - aspects of nature - in *Lucifer Rising* than have appeared in my films before - like there's sunrises and volcanoes and seascapes and wild animals - things I love - ruins - things I love.

You've described yourself, at various times, as mean and gloomy.

I'll admit to a certain amount of cosmic melancholy. I am a manic-depressive, though that's a self-diagnosis. I also have elation, good feelings, good times.

Is Lucifer Rising *an optimistic movie?*

It is. Look, my own take on Lucifer is that he is the god of light and colour - his name: Bringer of light - Lucem fero, the carrier of the torch. I don't see him as the devil at all. This is my personal take that come from gnosticism - and Crowley.

So your Lucifer, he's nothing to do with Satan?

No. It's not anything to do with Satan, but I realize I'm dealing with a subject that many people find inflammatory: I hope so! I'm not making crowd pleasers. I think Lucifer is a beautiful name, a beautiful concept. But you know, for someone so important - the cosmic villain - there's not much text devoted to him. I've read as much as I could. I've researched my subject. I like the texts where he calls himself 'Mas belo que Dios' - more beautiful than

God! And of course that arrogance and hubris condemned him to being kicked out of heaven. The Christians have painted themselves into a corner, because the truly profound religions, like Hinduism, accept the fact that there are gods and godesses and that they are very sacred but they must also be destructive and that this is the balance of nature: hurricanes, earthquakes, as well as flowers blooming and crops ripening.

So, Lucifer can be seen as a healthy spirit?

I call him bright Lucifer. All the colours. All the play of light. As an artist, it's just my own take. I see him like Milton saw Satan. In fact, it was Milton who created Satan. He didn't have much to go on from the Bible, but he created this magnificent text...the fallen angel...his vision...the vision of a blind man.

What's Kenneth Anger's vision of evil?

(Laughs) I once defined evil as motion pictures and I'm not ready to take that back. I think evil is something which is attractive, and compelling, a seduction into the unreal which is glamourous and ultimately unsatisfactory. I think all those things can be said about movies. I still love movies.

Thanks to Kenneth Anger for his time, patience, and hospitality during the making of this interview.

KENNETH ANGER : A FILMOGRAPHY

Unless otherwise noted, the films were conceived, directed and edited by Kenneth Anger. We have also included films in which Anger has appeared as an actor or which he figures as subject.

Those films marked with an asterisk are are all in distribution in Britain with the British Film Institute. This filmography is based on Robert A. Haller's in his *Kenneth Anger: A Monograph*, Mystic Fire Video, New York, 1980, with some additions provided by Rebekah Ward, based on her conversations with Anger.

BABY BURLESQUES

1934 (director unknown) Educational Films, Poverty Row Studios, Hollywood. Baby exploitation at its tackiest. Featuring caricatures of contemporary politicians and figures from Hollywood.

A MIDSUMMER NIGHT'S DREAM

1935, by Max Reinhardt and William Dieterle. Anger played the Changeling prince.

FIREWORKS*

1947, 14 minutes, tinted b/w, sound
Camera assistant: Chester Kessler, Music by Respighi Filmed in Hollywood. Cast: Kenneth Anger (Dreamer) Gordon Gray (First Sailor). Bill Seltzer (Second Sailor) Festival Prizes: Brussels, Cannes, Biarritz and Paris.
In Fireworks *I released all the explosive pyrotechnics of a dream. Inflammable desires dampened by day under the cold water of consciousness are ignited that night by the libertarian matches of sleep, and burst forth in showers of shimmering incandescence. These imaginary displays provide a temporary relief.*

- Kenneth Anger.

PUCE MOMENT *

1949, 6 minutes, color, sound.
Music by Jonathan Halper. Filmed in Hollywood. Cast: Yvonne Marquis (Star).
A fragment of the never-completed Puce Women.
Puce Moment *takes on a spicier meaning when 'I'm a Hermit' and 'Leaving My Old Life Behind' on the track are combined with the visuals of shimmering antique dresses and languishing Hollywood star. The obvious suggestion here is a renunciation of drag-dressing, an escape from the fetishization of costume and a climb 'out of the closet'.*

- Carel Rowe.

RABBIT'S MOON (LA LUNE DES LAPINS).*

1950, 7 minutes, tinted b/w, sound
Camera assistant: Tourjansky. Filmed in Paris. Cast: Andre Soubeyran (Pierrot), Claude Revenant (Harlequin), Nadine Valence (Columbine).
Not released until 1972, then in a 16 minutes version with a pop soundtrack. In 1979 the shorter 7 minute version with a soundtrack by Andy Arthur replaced the 1973 version.
Rabbit's Moon *clearly centers on one aspect of Anger's filmmaking, an aspect which is less obvious in his other films - the use of human motion as a means by which the intense inner life of his characters is externalized. The film is a testament to Anger's awareness that, in film, states which go beyond words - the unutterable and the unbearable - can be specifically communicated through human motion.*

-Amy Greenfield.

EAUX D'ARTIFICE*

1953 13 minutes, color
Camera assistant: Thad Lovett, Music by Vivaldi. Filmed in the gardens of the Villa D'Este, Tivoli (Italy). Cast: Marmilla Salvatorelli (Lady).
In Eaux D'Artifice *we see a baroque maze of staircases, fountains, gargoyles and balustrades. A figure in eighteenth century costume, flowing dress, and high headpiece hurries through this*

environment while the camera zooms into and away from the mask-like faces ,water spirits carved in stone ,or studies in slow motion the fall of fountains and sprays, then turns into a fountain, and her silhouetted form dissolves into an identical fountain arrangement.

- P. Adams Sitney.

INAUGURATION OF THE PLEASURE DOME*
1954, 38 minutes, color, sound
Camera assistant: Robert Straede. 'Sacred Mushroom Edition' has music by Janacek (Glagolithic Mass) Filmed in Hollywood. Cast: Samson DeBrier (Lord Shiva, Osiris, The Great Beast), Camerson (The Scarlet Woman, Kali), Katy Kadell (Isis), Renata Loome (Lilith), Anais Nin (Astarte), Paul Mathison (Pan), Curtis Harrington (Cesare the Somnambulist), Kenneth Anger (Hecate), Peter Loome (Ganymede).
Other versions had music by Harry Partch (41 minutes 1954-56), and the Electric Light Orchestra (38 minutes 1978). A 41 minute 1958 version was presented at Brussels on three screens.
Festival Prize: L'Age d'or Award, Brussels International Experimental Film Festival.

Dedicated to the few; and to Aleister Crowley; and the crowned and conquering child. — *Kenneth Anger*

The film is derived from one of Crowley's dramatic rituals where people in the cult assume the identity of a god or a goddess. In other words, it's the equivalent of a masquerade party - they plan this for a whole year and on All Sabbaths Eve they come as the gods and goddesses that they have identified with, and the whole thing is like an improvised happening.
This is the actual thing the film is based on. In which the gods and goddesses interact and in The Inauguration of the Pleasure Dome *it's the legend of Bacchus that's the pivotal thing and it ends with the god being torn to pieces by the Bacchates. This is the underlying thing. But rather than using a specific ritual, which would entail quite a lot of the spoken word as ritual does,*

I wanted to create a feeling of being carried into a world of wonder. And the use of color and phantasy is progressive; in other words, it expands, it becomes completely subjective - like when people take communion, and one sees it through their eyes.

- Kenneth Anger.

THE DEAD
1960, 11 minutes, silent
Directed by Stan Brakhage, filmed in Paris in the Pere Lachaise Cemetary. Brakhage used Anger to represent his own feelings of depression and frustration.

ARABESQUE FOR KENNETH ANGER
Directed by Marie Menken, 1961, 4 minutes, sound
Although Anger does not appear in the work, physically, he is present as an idea, as well as the subject of the film's dedication.

SCORPIO RISING*
1963 29 minutes, color, sound
Camera: Kenneth Anger. Music by Little Peggy March, The Angels, Bobby Vinton, Elvis Presley, Ray Charles, The Crystals, The Ran-Dells, Kris Jensen, Claudine Clark, Gene McDaniels, The Surfaris. Filmed in Brooklyn and Manhattan. Cast: Bruce Byron (Scorpio). Johnny Sapienza (Taurus), Frank Carifi (Leo). John Palone (Pinstripe). Ernie Allo (Joker), Barry Rubin (Fall Guy), Steve Crandell (Blondie), Bill Dorfmann (Back) Johnny Dodds (Kid).
Festival Awards: First Prize, Evian, France, 1966 Golden Cup, 11th Festival of Rapallo, Italy, 1965, First Prize, Third Annual Independent Film-Makers' Festival, Foothill College, CA. First Prize, Documentary, Poretta Terme Festival of Free Cinema, Italy, 1964

Dedicated to Jack Parsons, Victor Childe , Jim Powers, James Dean, T.E. Lawrence, Hart Crane, Kurt Mann, The Society of Spartans, The Hell's Angels, and all overgrown boys who will everyone of them follow the whistle of Love's brother.

- Kenneth Anger.

Kenneth Anger's emblematic film called Scorpio Rising (of course, a phallic metaphor) shows the intimate connection among Hell's Angelism, idolatrous sex, childish violence, and fascism. While some of the realistic space of Scorpio Rising is the open road, and we do indeed see militaristic Leather Boys speeding along, the symbolic space is a Leather Boy's bedroom den where he 'moons' amid the fetishes adorning his walls and reads comic books. The step from there to the open road is also symbolic in that, according to Anger, it involves a death wish - final release into infinite space. When, toward the end of Scorpio Rising, we see a group leader haranguing on a rostrum, we have an image of Hitlerian hysteria, urging youth on to sacrifice itself in death. Sexuality per se has been concretely transmuted and superseded. Death, not Sex, rides the motorcycle.

- Parker Tyler.

.... surely the most widely seen film in the history of the American avant-garde. WIth it's self-conscious media quotaitons, mock-heroic view of urban youth culture, knowing homoeroticism, and smashing use of rock'n'roll, Scorpio Rising burst dramatically on the American scene. If its acceptance was not completely universal -the Los Angeles Police Department confiscated the print during its initial midnight run, and Anger was sued by the American Nazi party for 'desecrating' the swastika - no other underground movie has ever had a comparable effect on Hollywood production. The Wild Angels, Midnight Cowboy, Easy Rider, Mean Streets, and American Graffiti can all be seen as part of its ripple effect.
Not the least important aspect of the film was Anger's dense, almost subliminal editing style. It's a truism that television commercials are heir to theories of Sergei Eisenstein, but I'd venture that Madison Avenue learned more about the power of associative montage from Scorpio Rising than The Battleship Potemkin. Although the rise of structuralism severely mitigated Anger's influence within the avant-garde of the early seventies, Scorpio Rising has the same relationship to the recent super-8 punk films as Gogol's Overcoat was said to have had on modern literature. Filmmakers Eric Mitchell, Beth and Scott B, and Vivienne Dick have, all in their own ways, come out of

Anger's leather jacket.
- Jim Hoberman, American Film, March 1981.

I well remember the first time I saw a Kenneth Anger film. It was about 1964 at Vernon Simmerman's loft downtown and Jonas Mekas showed us Scorpio Rising, after it was banned.
Of all his films, it is still the one I like the most. I was impressed by his ironic use of pop music and by his sense of rhythm. I was also fascinated by his ambiguous relationship to Hollywood, his love/hate continuously expressed through the use and abuse of Hollywood imagery, in a romantic, decadent mood.
There is a pagan religiosity in his films. His continuous reference to myth and to ritual creates a hypnotising, a dream atmosphere that seems to put the viewer in a state of trance. Kenneth Anger is a unique filmmaker, an artist of exceptional imagination.

- Martin Scorsese, 1989.

KUSTOM KAR KOMMANDOS*
1965, 3 minutes, color, sound
Camera assistant: Arnold Baskin, Music by the Parris Sister, Filmed in San Bernadino. Cast: Sandy Trent (Car Customiser). A fragment of a larger, never completed project
Kustom is an oneiric vision of a contemporary American (and specifically Californian) teenage phenomenon, the world of the hot-rod and customized car. I emphasized the word oneiric, as Kustom will not be a 'documentary' covering the mechanical hopping-up and esthetic costomizing of cars, but rather a dream-like probe into the psyche of the teenager for whom the unique aspect of the power-potentialized customized car represents a poetic extension of personality, an accessible means of wish-fulfillment.

-Kenneth Anger.

LUCIFER RISING
1966 Central footage of this first version stolen.

INVOCATION OF MY DEMON BROTHER*
(ARRANGEMENT IN BLACK AND GOLD).

1969, 11 minutes, color, sound
Camera: Kenneth Anger. Music by Mick Jagger (Moog synthesizer). Filmed in San Francisco at the Straight Theatre and the Russian Embasssy. Cast: Speed Hacker (Wand-bearer). Lenore Kandel (Deaconess). William Beutel (Deacon), Kenneth Anger (Magus), Van Leuven (Acolyte). Harvey Bialy (Brother), Timotha (Sister), Anton Szandor LaVey (Satan), Bobby Beausoleil (Lucifer). Made from the remains of the 1966 *Lucifer Rising* project.
Awards :   Tenth Independent Film Award (for the year 1969) by Film Culture.
For Anger the aesthetic endeavour is a category of magick. His image of the self is particularly complex because it involves as many distinctions as there are grades for the magician. Like Inauguration of the Pleasure Dome, *the vision of the self in* Invocation *has its foundation in the Romantic idea of the unitary man whose one character is made up of different individuals in opposition. But the magician of* Invocation *is of a higher order than Shiva of* Inauguration, *and the range of the film is both wider and more diffuse.*

- P. Adams Sitney.

HENRI LANGLOIS
1970 Directed by Hershon/Guerra. Details unknown.

LOOK BACK AT ANGER
1974 Directed by Leo Vale. Produced by Robert Haller. 12 minutes.
Both Anger and Haller dislike this film portrait. The film has Anger speaking about his own work intercut with stills from old movies and extracts from his films. Anger's discussion of the influence of the colour schemes from Aleister Crowley's Thoth Tarot deck on *Scorpio Rising* is, however, of particular interest.

LUCIFER RISING.*
1970-1980, 30 minutes, color, sound.
A presentation of Anita Pallenberg. Camera assistant: Michael Cooper. Music by Bobby Beausoleil and the Freedom Orchestra (Tracy Prison). Thelemic consultant: Gerald J Yorke. Filmed in Luxor, Karnak, Gizeh, Externsteine, London, Avebury. Cast: Miriam Gibril (Isis) Donald Cammell (Osiris), Haydn Couts (Adept), Kenneth Anger (Magus), Sir Francis Rose (Chaos), Marianne Faithfull (Lilith), Leslie Huggins (Lucifer). An earlier version carries a soundtrack by Jimmy Page.
Lucifer Rising *burns on a slower fuse than his earlier work: it strikes a balance between Eisensteinian montage (the relation of one image to another) and an interest in the 'spiritual' essence of individual images. The film provides its own metaphor for this balance in one of the introductory shots: a stream of molten lava crosses the land in the foreground, while the placid ocean stretches away in to the distance in the upper part of the frame. Fire and water imagery are similarly counterpointed throughout, as if* Fireworks *and* Eaux d'Artifice *had been brought together into mysterious union.*

-Tony Rayns.

Notes on the Hidden Cinema of Kenneth Anger

by Rebekah Wood

All of Anger's films are separate movements in one vast film, a large symphony in which all kinds of rituals occur   -Elliot Stein .

(Anger), the true cosmic explorer
                    -Jonas Mekas .

The film is the art of managing objects. It is the incarnation of the dream of its inventor... The film makes possible the realization of what cannot be realized in life.
                    -Dziga Vertov.

Cinema

Anger has maintained his position as enfant terrible of the avant-garde for forty years. Brought to the eye in sharp and scandalous confrontation from rigorously conceived sets of oppositions, Anger's films explore the world in a complex, visionary manner, one which consistently illuminates pure image and rises against the limitations of language.

Legend

Kenneth Anger, more than any other avant-garde film-maker is the conscious artificer of his own myth.   *-P. Adams Sitney.*

Film-maker, Magus, Occultist, Controversialist: an inextricable part of the Anger legend are the lost and finished films. Conversely, incident and detail which surround the lost work serve to compound the legend. Biographic and filmographic detail interact - a mutual dynamic. The lost films occur at crucial points in Anger's career and define major issues in avant-garde cinema: artistic (form and chaos under the rites of experimentation); and practical (finance, censorship, illegality).

Anger's precocious and non-prolific career remains partially hidden. Like Welles and Eisenstein, his progress is marked by aborted projects and appalling disappointments. Anger's films have been burnt, banned, lost, stolen, revised, withdrawn, sold to private collectors and, most frequently, disrupted for lack of means.

Resistance

More real than Anger, 'artificer' is the depth and complexity of Anger's cinema. Its absolute nature defies easy analytic or anecdotal dissemination. Anger has significantly altered some of his films to produce slight or radical change in meaning, increasing the irrational percept that the work has its autonomous life (an imaginistic viewing experience).

Anger's montage can be of such formidable complexity (multi-layer, non-synchronous transformations), it would be impossible to log an Anger film shot by shot. Anger's cinema-montage of attractions, conceived exactly as Eisenstein's - takes the spectator into psychological, emotional and intellectual spaces which are ineffable. The implications of Anger's arcane undertakings, his idealist's insistence on insight has decisive moral significance. His films are never the impersonal, exclusively esoteric product of the secret society, but an order in which the spectator takes his place.

Six Films Before Fireworks

I think that children generally do exert influence on their toys, that their choice is directed by inclinations and desires which, however vague and unformulated, are nevertheless very real. Still, I would not deny the contrary, that is to say, that toys act upon the child, particularly upon one with literary or artistic inclinations...

There is a kind of toy recently on the increase upon which I shall pronounce no judgement of value. I mean the scientific toy. Its principal defect is its high cost, but it can provide extended amusement and develop, within the child, the taste for surprising and wonderful effects .

- Baudelaire: La Morale de Joujou, 1859 .

It developed as a kind of hobby, even though I never looked on it as any kind of a lark. I took myself quite seriously as a child. I was going to make films and put my name of them: a film by Kenneth Anger

- Kenneth Anger, 1989.

Who Has Been Rocking My Dreamboat?

(1941, black and white, silent, 16mm, seven minutes, filmed in Santa Monica). Conceived, directed, photographed, edited by Kenneth Anger. Cast: neighbourhood children.

Summer before Pearl Harbour. Using rapid cross-cutting, the playworld of children shown over-shadowed by war. Newsreel holocaust flash-cuts cross their reverie. The children stop playing and fall to the ground in mock death. Smoke billows over the still bodies.

Tinsel Tree

(1942, black and white, silent, 16mm, three minutes, filmed in Santa Monica). Conceived, directed, photographed, edited by Kenneth Anger.

Using hand-coloured over-tint, ritual burning of the family Christmas tree. From close-up: branches decked with baubles and tinsel to stripping and burning the tree. Scarlet and gold coloration.

Prisoner of Mars

(1942, black and white, silent, 16mm, eleven minutes, filmed in Santa Monica). Conceived, directed, photographed, edited by Kenneth Anger. Camera assistant, Charles Vreeland. Minatures and costumes by Kenneth Anger. Cast: Kenneth Anger - the boy elect from earth. First formal use of serial-chapter aesthetic. Science fiction rendition of the minotaur myth. Anger 'chosen... boy of the future' rocketed to Mars, lands in a labyrinth littered with the bones of previous travellers.

The Nest

(1942, black and white, silent, 16mm, twenty minutes, filmed in Santa Monica). Conceived, directed, photogrqaphed, edited by Kenneth Anger. Cast: Bob Jones (brother); Jo Wittaker (sister); Dare Harris (later John Derek, boyfriend).

A precocious study of latent eroticism. Signalling to one another with mirrors, a perfect brother and sister commune. A third party arrives to interfere. Harmony is broken. Violence ensues.

Escape Episode

(1944, black and white, silent, later re-edited with sound in 1946, music by Scriabin, 16mm, thirty minutes, filmed in Los Angeles). Conceived, directed, photographed, edited by Kenneth Anger. Cast: Marilyn Granas (the girl); Bob Jones (the boy); Nora Watson (the guardian).

An experimental study showing a conflict of moral values. Set in a decaying stucco-gothic seaside church. Free adaptation of the Andromeda myth. Following the psychology of the protagonist, a sensitive adolescent girl, the film becomes increasingly subjective. Stifled by the hand of religious fanaticism, the girl encounters a 'nature boy', Perseus of the beach. The pair conspire to break parental bonds. Premiered at the Coronet Theatre, Hollywood, 1947.

Drastic Demise

(1945, black and white, using negative insert, silent, 16mm, five minutes, filmed in Hollywood). Conceived, directed, photographed, edited by Kenneth Anger. Cast: anonyous American crowd.
Hand-held camera plunged into the 'sexually turned-on' crowds of V. J. Day. Argument constructed, negative versus positive image - hysteria of a euphoric Hollywood Boulevard crowd. Marking the ambivalence of V. J. Day with a mushroom-cloud-end: the end of the war; the birth of the atomic age. An accompanying original score for percussion. *Escape Episode, Drastic Demise, Fireworks* were featured at the San Franciso Museum of Modern Art, and offered as a package for rental, 1947.

Emanations

The cinematic art of Anger has been intensely ritualistic since *Fireworks.* From what remains - anecdotal description - a picture of an aesthetic emerges. Elements, fragments of ritual and idea make toward central concerns to be refined by Anger's ascetic deliberation. Anger's absorption with psycho-drama is clear. Narrative direction through the transformation of myth, archetype and ritual action. Emphasis on human interaction: sexuality, coercion, power relations (*The Nest*). Inception of Anger's morally disconcerting universe. Tension between fact and fiction, reality and dream. Film as the intermediate zone between subjective experience and external event (*Who has been Rocking my Dreamboat?*).

Two figures arise. First: Anger, his own best organizer, bringing will to bear. The creation of form, fulfillment of fantasy. Construction of a child's world - ideal, retreat from strict rearing (*Escape Episode*). Second: The Seeker, rebellious, heart-troubled, perpetual adolescent - in Pierrot, Scorpio, Sandy and Anger himself as Magus on film. Of dual significance: fictional and mythographic figures are biographic projections in this respect.

In clear focus: Anger's thraldom to the fantastical, here classical myth and science fiction. The 'external recurrence of myth and archetype, an irrationalistic doctrine, always relevant, is extensively present in Anger's films: *Prisoner of Mars, Escape Episode, Rabbit's Moon, Inauguration of the Pleasure Dome* - and consummately in *Lucifer Rising,* the forever boyhood of science fiction. Science Fiction is the fantastical meeting ground of archaic myth and modernist aspiration.

Inauguration of the Pleasure Dome

Melies' *Voyage dans la Lune*

The artist believes in the future because he is part of it.
-Modest Mussorgsky.

Affinity to this genre points to another of the creative collisions inherent in Anger's cinema: the anomoly of ancient vision and rigorous modernity -the genre dedicated to make-believe, source of persistent technical innovation - Anger's cinema.

Melies prepared many early Science Fiction films... A Trip to the Moon 1902), set the criteria for future Science Fiction efforts, clearly identifying the necessary attributes for an excellent Science Fiction production - good story, creative special effects, precise cinematography and a generous supply of imagination . *-Forrest Ackerman,*
A Reference Guide to Ameerican Science Fiction FiIms, Vol. I.

Specific images recur. The ritualized burning of the Christmas tree returns in *Fireworks;* the act of ritual self-preparation (ablutions and mirrors) in *The Nest* will mark *Puce Moment, Scorpio Rising* and *Kustom Kar Kommandos.* The mirror-signals of the perfect pair in *The Nest* reappear: Isis and Osiris signalling across a red desert in *Lucifer Rising. Who Has Been Rocking My Dreamboat?* and *Invocation of My Demon Brother* show private worlds threated by war; perpetual violence and chaos.

Magic

The cinema is essentially the revealer of a whole occult life with which it puts us into direct contact
                                                    - Antonin Artaud.

The Love that Whirls
(1949, colour, no other credits available)

The Love that Whirls *was inspired by Frazer's* The Golden Bough *and was about a human sacrifice- specifically an Aztec ritual in which a youth is chosen to be king. It's about symbolic Kingship. After one year, the day comes when the King is sacrificed. When his time is up, his flutes are broken and there is a ritual. I found this a compelling situation, but the film had a few glimpses of nudity, which at that time simply wasn't done, even though the context of the nudity made it clear that it was nothing to do with lewdness and obscenity. The film was Kodachrome and had to be developed at the Eastman-Kodak processing plant. Kodak ended up keeping it, saying that they couldn't allow their film to be used for nudity!*
                                                    - Kenneth Anger 1989.

Thelema Abbey
(1955, black and white , sound, 16mm, ten minutes, filmed in Thelema Abbey, Cefalu, Sicily).

I have made one documentary: Thelema Abbey. *This was about Aleister Crowley's erotic frescos. The film was made for Houlton Television which was a branch of 'Picture Post' an extinct British magazine. They lost it. I've tried to find it and it's untraceable. I lived in Crowley's house, alone, but that kind of thing doesn't bother me. I had to. It was the only way to get it done. I spent three months there scraping the whitewash, which had turned to stone, off the walls. It was a big job, but one of the most exciting things I have ever done. They were still there - all those hyper-psychedelic murals: goblins and demons in fabulous colour, scarlet and pumpkin-red. Actually they were good paintings, similar in feel to Ensor .*
                                                    - Kenneth Anger, 1989.

Corollaries

Magic, labyrinthine in its connection. Anger has claimed magick his life-work, the camera his magickal weapon. A magical scale resonates in the work and can be understood in many ways: -

Governing Magick - Aleister Crowley. Crowley's principles of nature and thought have esoteric value, rich inferences for the initiate - 'follow me into the flower called nowhwere'. More real, Crowley's work through Anger's work is an 'open' system, an ordering in process, of infinite extension, not superstitious limitation. Crowley's theorems are at once original and the superlative syntheses of many alternative systems: metaphysical, alchemical (through alchemic, chemical and scientific), occult, astrologic, magical. Anger's legerdemain with Crowley's magickal doctrine is his medium for categorization/deliberation on infinite universal possibility.

Man is ignorant of his nature , of his own being and power. Even his idea of his limitations is based on experience of the past; and every step in progress extends his empire. There is therefore no reason to assign theoretical limits to what he may be or what he may do .
                        - Aleister Crowley, Magick in Theory and Practice.

Magic, the antecedent of a scientific sensibility, thus antecedes cinema-science. Cinema has its own fundamental science. Magic and Science mark cinema's inception: the transforming tricks of Melies, deceptive fictions, depend equally on the skill of the prestidigiteur and on scientific empiricism.

Cameron as the Scarlet Woman and Samson De Brier as the Great Beast in *Inauguration of the Pleasure Dome,* 1954.

Magicians have been falsely considered lunatics. So have those that project dreams that come scientifically true.
- Parker Tyler, Underground Film.

Strong Magic - implications for the person; self-magic of the Magus.
In so far as religion assumes the world to be directed by concious agents who may be turned from their purpose by persuasion, it stands in fundamental antagonism to magic as well as to science both of which take for granted that the source of nature is determined, not by the passion of personal being, but by the operation of immutable laws.
- Frazer (on the poetic magician), The Golden Bough.

Crowley's magick stands in opposition to the caprice of one supra-being, asserting *magick as the Science and Art of causing change to occur in conformity to the will.*

Every intentional act is a magical act - Aleister Crowley.

Making movies is casting spells - Kenneth Anger.

On film, Anger performs as Magus. The circle, which includes the spectator, seals.

The greatest of sorcerers would be the one who could cast a spell on himself to the degree of taking his own phantomasgora for autonomous apparitions .
- Juan Luis Borges, The Circular Ruins.

Magic and Cinema - poetic Method. The suggestive nature of metaphor brings unknown, occult (hidden), unexpected relationships. Content is made graphic/visible, understood - a materiality best suited to film.

Meta - change for:-
Any required change may be effected by the application of the proper kind and degree of force in the proper manner, through

Anger as the Magus in *Invocation of My Demon Brother.*

the proper medium...
-Aleister Crowley, Magic in Theory and Practice..

Anger's cinema - metaphors, flirtations, not allusion, reminder, or analogy, but with an aspect of each of Anger's poetic manners - personal, provocative, a procession of exaggerations and intensifications with the black brilliance of macabre fantasy - Anger's magic(k)al atmospheres and illuminations.

Paris

Between 1950 and 1961 Anger lived in Paris. There he attempted three astoundingly ambitious film projects: based on Jean Cocteau's *Le Jeune Homme et la Mort*, Lautreamont's *Maldoror* and Pauline Reage's *L'Histoire d'O.*

The surrealists Breton and Soupault hailed Lautreamont as a forefather who, with Baudelaire and Rimbaud, was part of an unholy trinity of genius. This revolutionary classic [Maldoror] remained truly an 'underground' work, little discussed and less read .

- Alexis Lykiard, translator of Maldorer.

Unnoticed on first publication (Paris 1868), by the end of the century it had become a cause celebre. *Maldoror:* an epic-poetic testament reveals a shrouded twilight world, half-ecstasy, half-nightmare of angels, grave diggers, madmen and perverted children.

The Story of O was a notorious underground classic - a rare example of pornography sublimated to art. It first appeared via clandestine circulation in Paris, 1954.
Neither a fantasy nor a case history, with its alternate beginnings and endings; its simple direct style (that of a fable); its curious air of abstraction, of indpendence from time, place and personality, it resembles a legend - the spiritual history of a saint or martyr ... the story gradually opens out into a Daedalian maze of perverse relations - a clandestine society of formality and elegance, where the primary bond is mutual complicity in dedication to the pleasures of sadism and masochism.
-New York Times Review.

Le Jeune Homme et la Mort

1951, black and white, silent, 16mm, filmed in Paris. Cast: Jean Babilee (young man); Nathalie Philipart (death). From Jean Cocteau's 1947 ballet, of the same title.
The first few months after I arrived in Paris, I was fortunate enough to see, at the Theatre Champs Elysees, a wonderful performance of Jean Cocteau's Le Jeune Homme et La Mort *danced by the original cast of Nathalie Phillipart and Jean Babilee. The ballet was set to Bach's* Passacaglia. *The set was a beautiful backdrop of the Paris skyline in the 1920's. I discussed*

the ballet with Cocteau and told him I'd like to film it. He gave me permission and wrote me a letter to find a producer - saying that he had full confidence and wanted me to direct it. I went round, approaching some of the big names like Pauvert. Despite the fact I had Cocteau's name, my budget was too high. I never found a producer. I wanted to film in 35mm, technicolour with a sound stage. I managed to shoot a 16mm, black and white study-film. Just to have light, I filmed in Jean Babilee's garden. The young man hangs himself from a tree. It was winter - cold, every movement was accompanied by visible breath from the chill air. When death comes to take the young man, she is wearing a mask and stills -like the image of death in Orphee. *I'm sorry I couldn't find backing. It would have been a classic - rented forever.*
-Kenneth Anger, 1989.

Maldoror

(Details unknown)
I discovered the book when I was quite young. I loved it, put a lot of passion into it. I found people to play the parts, I found settings, gaslit corners, places that still had the romantic look of a Second Empire. It was a terrific ambition to make this epic film-poem. I found ways to translate the text's extraordinary images. I planned to film a mid-19th century story taking place in 20th century Paris. I filmed 'the hymn to the ocean', on the beach at Deauville, with Rosella Hightower and members of the Marquis de Cuevas Ballet. They danced in the sea, tables were placed beneath the water line so the dancers could stand on their points. It looked as it they were standing on waves. The people who called themselves 'surrealists' were furious - this group of punks threatened me - they didn't want a Yank messing round with their sacred text. I just told them to go to hell!
I also managed to film the war of the flies and pins. I put bags of pins and dozens of flies into a glass container; revolved the container and filmed in close-up. As the pins dropped, the flies zig-zagged to escape. In slow-motion, an impressive image. That was about it. You can't conjure up a movie, unless you have money.

-Kenneth Anger, 1989.

Kenneth Anger and the Rebellious Angels. Photomontage by Teske, 1954.

L'Histoire d'O

L'Histoire d'O

1961, black and white, silent, 16mm, 20 minutes, filmed in Paris. From Pauline Reage's book *L'Histoire d'O*, 1954. *To help finance my stay in Paris, I wrote* Hollywood Baby-lone *and J J Pauvert published it. He also published* L'Histoire d'O, *an elegantly written sado-masochistic fairytale, very dreamlike and totally implausible. I thought it could make an interesting experimental film. I got permission to do it and I had some money - but not enough to see the whole thing through. I was helped by the boyfriend of the girl playing 'O'. It turned out that his money was bounty from the kidnapping of Eric Peugeot - grandson of the auto magnate. I knew nothing about this. I found out in a very abrupt manner. The yound man was arrested and I was questioned about the money being used for my film. The young lady playing 'O' was the daughter of a minister. Her parents knew nothing about her being in the film and when they did find out filming came to an instant halt.*

- Kenneth Anger, 1989.

Inferences

The poetics and metaphysics of symbolism mark cinema's inception. Anger's cinema draws from liberal literary form. His stay in Paris compounded an extensive knowledge of fin-de-siecle literature. His work has an affinity with romantic symbolism: nuance over ratiocination, sensibility over logic; the decadent ethos of elaborate vicissitude, emblem and hyperbole. French romantic symbolism creates its own labyrinthine enigmas: both prophecy and satire intensely involved with subject yet critical of its own limits. Symbolism reminds itself of its own affected limitations and fetishistic downfall, a form which favours arguing with itself and includes its predecessors.

Anger's sojourn in Paris involved an artistic realignment. Like Cocteau, like Lautreamont, Anger's *Fireworks* marks an extreme positioning: Anger, as the son of his own work, a self-engendering; ill-constructed as narcissim.

This doubling: Ducasse's *Lautreamont* Cocteau's *Magic Mirror*, Anger's *Magick Lantern* and public work as Magus, is a self-engendering which usurps the family.

I am my son, my father, my mother and myself.

-Antonin Artaud

Finis

Anger's works contain the key to their own elucidation in the form of clear parallelisms between his films; direct and indirect connection to definite metaphysical, magickal and artistic contexts within which he has elected to situate himself. Once these connections have been made they may as easily be eschewed: his style, rarity of vision and complexity of thought are indelibly original.

His cinema is filled with disordering passions. It is also scientifically cool and technically precise. The singularity of his ideas drives through the most co-operative of arts. His perfectionism of image defies avant-garde economy. Anger's is a supra-effort of concentration to transmute self, in the spirit of the translator, medium, recorder and magician, into a universal art. Non-prolific, non compromising, Anger has endured.

Rabbit's Moon

A Salacious Footnote

Senators in Bondage

(1976, Colour, sound, 16mm, $1,776)

The Eisenstein of Satanism strikes again! Prints of Kenneth Anger's first limited edition Senators in Bondage *The master negative will be sealed; no further prints will be struck. Edition strictly limited to 13 copies in honour of the 13 original colonies. Each print individually hand-coloured, supplied in a red, white and blue box, bound in chain.* Senators in Bondage *movie metaphor of mighty eminences brought low. A vitriolic bon-bon concocted with malice; a curio for this bicentennial year .*

-Abby Hirsch publications, New York, June, 1976.

Matelots en Menottes

(1977, Colour, sound, 16mm, $1,200)

Matelots en Menottes - *a return to the orginal subject of* Fireworks. *Kenneth Anger's second limited edition. Edition strictly limited to 12 copies.*

-Abby Hirsch Publications. New York, June 1977.

Denunciation of Stan Brakhage

(1979) Confirmed by Jonas Mekas, no other details.

Mouse Heaven

(1987, colour, 16mm)

Scheduled for completion summer 1989; abandoned due to financial difficulties, no longer a work in progress. *Mouse Heaven* (a working title) based on Disney's original character (1928-1938). Planned as a fantastical collage. Faced with a gamut of marching Mickeys, the spectator would lose all perspective; using models, prints and original footage.

Hollywood Babylon

The movie! Negotiations in progress.

Anger and the star of *Mouse Heaven*, 1989. Photo: Kabbaz.

AN EXHAUSTIVELY SELECTIVE BIBLIOGRAPHY

Periodicals

Mayoux, Michel
Trois Creatures: Preamble a un Cinema Poetique.
Cahiers du Cinéma, No. 10, 1952

Mekas, Jonas
The Experimental Film in America.
[Filmography under 'The Most Representative American Film Poets' at end of article.]
Film Comment, May-June, 1955.

Edwards, Roy
Le Lautreamont du Cinema.
Objectif, No. 4, January 1961.

Kelman, Ken
Thanatos in Chrome.
Film Culture, No. 31, Winter 1963.

Micha, Rene
Le Nouveau Cinema.
Les Temps Modernes, No. 214, 1964.

Cooke, Alan
Free Cinema
Sequence, No. 13, 1965.

Dientsfrey, Harris
Two Films and an Interlude by Kenneth Anger.
Artforum, New York, 1965.

Brown, Kenneth
Aux Portes de la Nuit.
Lettres Françaises, No. 1101, October 1965.
[Erudite review of *Scorpio Rising.*]

Cornwell, Regina
On Kenneth Anger.
December, Vol. 10, 1968.

Rayns, Tony
Lucifer, A Kenneth Anger Kompendium
Cinema (Britain), No. 4, October 1969.

Landow, George
Kenneth Anger.
Afterimage, No. 2, Autumn, 1970.

not known

Le Cinema Underground.
Actuel, No. 3, December, 1970.
Filmography, discussion of psychodrama and psychic delirium.

Morin, Jaques

Kenneth Anger: s'adresser d'abord à l'oeil.
Cinema 72, No. 165, April, 1970.
[Review of Anger's films.]

Unattributed

Filmography.
Film Dope, No. 1, December, 1972.

Scorel, Stephane

Programme Underground.
Telecine, No. 179, June, 1973.
[Review of programme of Anger, Kuchar and Nelson films].

Erskine, Robert

J. Vaughn Loves K. Anger.
Time Out, No. 179, 27 July - 2 August, 1973.

Unattributed

Anger Breaks.
Time Out, No. 180, 3 - 9 August, 1973.

Rowe, Carel

Illuminating Lucifer.
Film Quarterly, Vol. 27, No. 4, Summer, 1974.

Alexander, Kent Thomas

San Francisco's Hipster Cinema.
Cineaste, Vol. 7, No. 1, 1975.

Pacadis, Alain

Kenneth Anger à l'Olympic.
Libération, February 10, 1976.

Marcorelles, Louis

Cinema Kenneth Anger à l'Entrepot.
Le Monde, February 27, 1976.
[Review of The Magick Lantern Cycle and underground cinema of the 1950's and 1960's.]

Martin, Marcel

Tout Kenneth Anger.
Ecran, No. 45, March, 1976.

Hoberman, Jim

Sympathy for the Devil.
American Film, Vol. 6, No. 5, March, 1981.

Wees, William

Preternatural Light in the Films of Kenneth Anger.
Cinetracts, Vol. 5, No. 1, Summer, 1982.

Rayns, Tony

The Elusive Lucifer.
Monthly Film Bulletin, Vol. 49, No. 584, September, 1982.

Truman, James

A Look Back at Anger.
The Face, No. 39, July, 1983.

Johnstone, Paul

Correspondence between Anger and Paul Johnstone, 1947 - 1949.
Film Culture, No. 70/71, 1983.

Mayoux, Michel

Kenneth Anger.
Le Cinéma, Vol. 6, Atlas, Paris, 1983.
[Discussion of Anger's erotic, esoteric and aesthetic obsessions.]

Witte, Kirstin

Fetisch-Messen.
Frauen und Film, No. 38, May 1985.
[On Anger's use of costume as fetish]

Unattributed

Biofilmography.
Film Dope, No. 39, March, 1988.
[Update on previous biofilmography]

Interviews with Kenneth Anger

Spider Magazine

An Interview with Kenneth Anger
Film Culture, No. 40, Spring, 1966. Reprinted from Spider Magazine.

Wasserman, John

Witchcraft by Anger.
The San Francisco Chronicle, September 30, 1966.

Martin, Bruce and Medjuck, Joe

Kenneth Anger.
Take One, Vol. 1, No. 6, 1967.
Making a movie is like casting a spell.

Burton, Shelley

Conversation with Kenneth Anger.
Los Angeles Free Press, March 10, 1967.
Vietnam: the establishment's way of masturbating young boys' violence.

Pye, Michael

Occult and Ritual Images.
The Scotsman, September 15, 1969.

Oakes, Philip

Light Up a Lucifer
The Sunday Times, April 12, 1970.

Cott, Jonathan

Anger Rising.
The Sunday Remparts, May 7, 1970.
A demon is a convenient way of labelling a force, the demons I'm working with in Lucifer are what magicians call 'elementals'.

Rayns, Tony

Aleister Crowley and Merlin Magick.
Friends, No. 14, September, 1970.

Parkin, Molly

Pretty Sexy and Satanic.
The Sunday Times, January 17, 1971.

Rayns , Tony

Dedication to Create Make Believe.
Time Out, No. 91, November, 1971.
....stare for eternity at your own head, mouthing back at you all the bad things you've allowed yourself to be quoted saying.

Baldwin, Neil

Kenneth Anger: Scorpio Rises Again.
Changes, No. 83, July, 1973.
I hardly ever show my films for free.

Turran, Kenneth

Kenneth Anger's Magic Quest.
American Film, Vol. 1, No. 6, 1976.
I see myself as a bit of a loner...I've never tried to play a role.

Martin, Marcel

Avec Kenneth Anger.
Ecran, No. 46, April, 1976.

Brown, Mick

Hollywood Anger.
Crawdaddy, September, 1976.
The underground film-maker's art is finally a precarious one and reputations don't pay the rent.

Calendo, John

Kenneth Anger Rising.
Oui, October, 1976.

Baker, Robb

The Trials of Lucifer.
SoHo Weekly News, October 28, 1976.
Lucifer: *it's been a continuing drama but I don't take any particular stance on it. I'm on top of it and I knew that sooner or later it would all work out.*

Bardach, Ann

Hollywood Bohemian: Kenneth Anger.
Wet, Vol. 4, No. 5, 1980.
I have to be independent. I've been that way since I was a kid. There were lots of no's and won't's. I continue that way.

Landis, William

Anger: Film's Rudest Boy.
SoHo News, July 16, 1980.
Eaux d'Artifice: *This teenager became a cardinal through no fault of his own. He loved swishing around in big red capes and hats, he built Tivoli with church money which he had siphoned off.*

English, Jack

Fire & Brimstone.
Time Out, No. 572, 1981.
Which contemporary film-makers do you respect?   - None.

Hardy, Robin and Wade, Michael

Kenneth Anger, Master in Hell.
Body Politic, No. 82, April, 1982.
The borderline between what is underground culture and what pop is shrouded in mist, but there is frequently traffic back and forth.

English, Jack

A Profile of Kenneth Anger.
On Film (US), Summer, 1983
[On Anger's attitudes to audiences, views on filmmaking].

McKenna, Kristine

The Gilded Palace of Sin.
New Musical Express, April 13, 1985.

Ashum, Dale

Interview with Kenneth Anger.
Pandemonium, Cambridge, Massachusetts, 1986.
My family was what people hardly believed existed: a family of Hollywood puritans...no picture shows on Sundays.

Writing by Kenneth Anger

Modestie at Art du Film

Cahiers du Cinéma, No. 5, September, 1951.
[Highly informative article on Anger's views about the nature of poetic cinema and inspiration.]

L'Olympe, ou le comportement des dieux.

Cahiers du Cinéma, No. 76, November, 1957.
[On the death of Hollywood, Rudolph Valentino, Thomas H. Ince, and the Arbuckle scandal.]

Hollywood ou le comportement des mortels.

Cahiers du Cinéma, No. 77, December, 1957.
[The demise of W. F. Murnau (not featured in the English version of Hollywood Babylon), Jean Harlow, Judy Garland, Thelma Todd.]

Aux Enfers.

Cahiers du Cinema, No. 79, January, 1958.
[Continuation of previous articles, with particular reference to the scandal magazine 'Confidential'.]

Hollywood Babylone.

Published by J. J. Pauvert, Paris, 1959.

A History of Eroticism.

Adapted from the French edition, Bibliothèque Internationale d'Erotologie; Published by J.J. Pauvert, Paris, 1961.

The Erotic Art of Bobby Beausoleil.

Puritan. (No other reference)

Atlantis: The Lost Continent.

Dover Press, Canada. (No date given)

Hollywood Babylon.

Straight Arrow Books, San Francisco, 1975.

In Memoriam; Henry Langlois.

Film Comment, Vol. 13, No. 2, March, 1977.

Hollywood Babylon II.

E.P. Dutton, New York, 1984.

Letter to the Editor: Concerning the Maya Deren Awards.	**Village Voice**; reprinted in **Motion Picture**, No. 3, 1987.
A Short Review of Close Encounters of the Third Kind.	**Film Comment**, Vol. 14, No. 1, January, 1978.

Books

Battcock, Gregory, editor	*The New American Cinema.* E. P. Dutton, New York, 1967.
Renan, Sheldon	*The Underground Film.* Studio Vista, New York, 1968.
Tyler, Parker	*Underground Film: A Critical History.* Grove Press, New York, 1969.
Sitney, P. Adams	*The American Independent Film.* Boston Museum of Fine Arts, Boston, 1971.
Mekas, Jonas	*Movie Journal: The Rise of the New American Cinema 1959 - 1971.* Collier Books, New York, 1972.
Durgnat, Raymond	*Sexual Alienation in the Cinema.* Studio Vista, London, 1974.
Dwoskin, Steve	*Film Is...* Overlook Press, New York, 1975.
Sitney, P. Adams	*The Essential Cinema: Essays on the the Films in the Collection of Anthology Film Archives.* New York University Press, New York, 1975.
Adams, P. Adams	*The Avant-Garde Film: A Reader of Theory and Criticism.* New York University Press, New York, 1978.
Sitney, P. Adams	*Visionary Film: The American Avant-Garde 1943 - 1978.* Oxford University Press, Oxford, 1979.

Rowe, Carel   *The Baudelairean Cinema: A Trend within the American Avant-Garde.*
                          UMI Research Press, Michigan, 1982.

James, David   *Allegories of Cinema: American Film in the 1960's.*
                          Princeton University Press, New Jersey, 1989.

Background Reading

Bessy, Maurice   *Imprécis d'Eroticisme.*
                          J.J. Pauvert, Paris, 1961.

Duca, Lo   *L'Erotisme au Cinéma.*
                          J.J. Pauvert, Paris, 1961.

Nin, Anais   *The Diary of Anaïs Nin 1955 - 1966.*
                          Harcourt, Brace, Jovanovich, New York, 1967.

Capote, Truman   *Music for Chameleons.*
                          Sphere Books, London, 1975.

Heide , Robert   *The Wonderful World of Movie Memorabilia.*
                          Doubleday, New York, 1986.

Friedrich, Otto   *City of Nets.*
                          Headline Books, Britain, 1987.

Compiled largely by Rebekah Wood, to whom many thanks, with additional information from BFI Library Services.